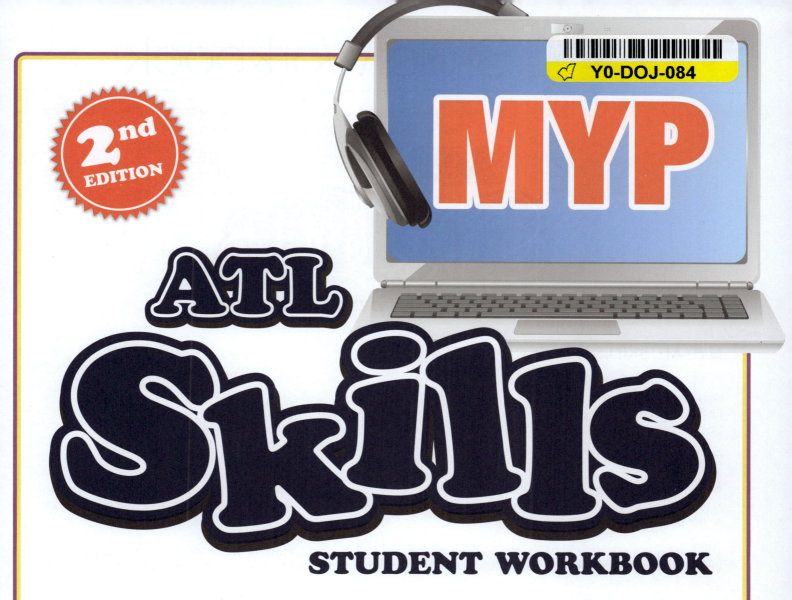

2nd EDITION

MYP

ATL Skills

STUDENT WORKBOOK

Contributor

MICK WALSH

Mick Walsh has been a leading and innovative educator, author and coach across Australasia and internationally for many years. His focus is on empowering teachers and school leaders to enter into meaningful dialogue about their core business of learning, teaching and building student and teacher wellbeing to enable collective beliefs, expectations and practices. He is keenly sought after to present at conferences and coach in schools on effectively implementing Positive Education and Wellbeing. To support teachers and school leaders to build both student and staff wellbeing, he authored the Learning Curve Positive Education Wellbeing program. The program is used by over 1000 schools world-wide.

MYP ATL SKILLS WORKBOOK

ISBN: 978-0-6482528-0-1
First published 2016
Second edition 2018

© Lance King and Print & Marketing Services (Vic) Pty Ltd 2018

The author and publisher have made all efforts to ensure accuracy and completeness of the information contained in this publication. However, no responsibility can be accepted for any errors and inaccuracies that occur and any loss or damage suffered as a result.

Lance King – The Art of Learning (2000) Ltd, New Zealand

Print & Marketing Services (Vic) Pty Ltd
79 Asling Street
Brighton VIC 3186
Australia

www.atlskills.com

Introduction

STUDENT WORKBOOK

READ THIS FIRST!

In this book you will find 93 ATL skills exercises. Each exercise has been designed to enable you to practice and get better at one small aspect of learning in general. The aim of this book is to help you to improve your own success – however you define success.

ATL skills exercises need to be practiced the same way you might practice a lay-up in basketball or an ollie on a skateboard or a new song on a musical instrument. First you work out exactly how to do it well and then you do it over and over again making small improvements every time until you've got it. And you will know you've "got it" when you can do it without thinking about it and maybe you are even good enough to teach someone else.

NO-ONE NEEDS TO GET GOOD AT **ALL** THESE SKILLS!!!

Your teachers will probably get together and select the exercises that they think will help improve any student's performance at school and then ask you to do these exercises in different classes. That will work fine but you can also do lots of these exercises by yourself or with a friend.

Each exercise gives you an activity to perform to practice the skill and it also gives you what is called a "Mastery" statement. This is a definition of what someone who was really, really good at this particular skill would be able to do. You can use this statement as a goal – something to aim for.

First you need to work out what you want to achieve (see *Achieving Goals* – pages 74-76), and then look for the specific skills that might help with that. If it is school work – what do you have trouble with – what might help you improve? Is it making good notes in class? See page 33 – *Note-making*. Is it meeting deadlines? See page 70 – *Deadlines*. And if that is the case, you might also need to look at page 90 and learn some *Perseverance* skills and maybe page 98 and learn how to deal with *Pressure and Stress*.

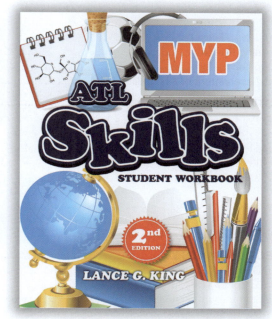

Do you get the idea?

This book is a self-help manual for all the skills you need to succeed – however you want to succeed.

And don't forget to send me feedback on which exercises you like the best and which ones were the most helpful – email me directly at lance@taolearn.com

Have fun!

Lance King

Table of Contents – by Cluster

ATL Skills

STUDENT WORKBOOK

Table of Contents – by Theme

ATL Skills STUDENT WORKBOOK

COMMUNICATION SKILLS

Communication involves the movement of information through written words (e.g. printed or digital media such as books, blogs, magazines, websites, emails, messaging), images (e.g. video, pixt, film, logos, maps, charts or graphs), digital data (to make connections between all your devices possible) and non-verbally through movement, gesture, tone and pitch of voice as well as through taste and smell.

Communication is not something that only human beings do. All animals communicate, computer systems communicate, your phone communicates. In this ATL skill cluster we are going to focus on the communication of knowledge and understanding between people.

Practicing the skills in this cluster will improve your critical reading, your understanding of your schoolwork and all your writing. You will learn the best ways to make notes in class and for when you are studying as well as the best way to write all your essays, reports and other assignments. You will also learn how to convey messages effectively, both verbally and non-verbally, and how to design and deliver great presentations that capture attention.

GREAT COMMUNICATIONS

The Rosetta Stone. On this stone, in 196BC, a new law from King Ptolemy of Egypt was inscribed for all his subjects to read. The thing that makes this one of the most famous "communications" ever is that the decree was written in three languages – Ancient Egyptian hieroglyphs, Demotic script and Ancient Greek.

In 1799, when the Rosetta Stone was discovered, ancient Greek was already mostly understood by archeologists and historians but Egyptian hieroglyphs were not, even though many thousands of examples had been found.

The Rosetta Stone enabled the translation of Ancient Egyptian hieroglyphs into Ancient Greek and then into modern languages which enabled giant leaps in understanding to be achieved.

Feedback

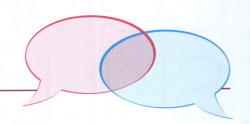

1.1a, 2m – Give and receive meaningful feedback.

Mastery

You will know you are at the **Expert** level in the use of this ATL skill when you can listen to, accept and respond appropriately to any type of feedback from any person.

Feedback means messages you receive from other people about how they perceive you. Sometimes those messages are positive, sometimes they are completely neutral and sometimes they are about things they think you could change. The purpose of giving and receiving feedback is improving performance.

This ATL skill is all about learning to deal well with all forms of feedback from others.

Exercise 1 – Verbal Feedback

a) Make up three lists of types of feedback – what would be a way you could say something to someone that you think would be seen as positive feedback, what could you say that would be more neutral and what could you say that would be seen as change feedback? Write in several examples of each.

1 e.g. I like, I enjoyed, I ...

2 e.g. I see, I agree with, I ...

3 e.g. I don't understand, I need, I ...

Exercise 2 – Giving Feedback on Written Work

a) Sit with a partner and swap your workbooks or your written notes in your subject.

b) What you are going to do is look at your partner's written work and give them feedback on what they have written or how they have written it or what the pages look like and then you are going to listen to their feedback on your work.

c) IMPORTANT!! The **only** acceptable response to any type of feedback is to say "thank you." Nothing else. You are not going to explain, defend or justify yourself, you are just going to say "thank you."

d) Person A goes first and says one thing that they like about Person B's work.

e) Person B says "thank you," then Person B says one thing they like about Person A's work.

f) Person A says "thank you."

g) Both write down what the feedback was in the Notes section on this page.

h) Repeat the same exercise giving neutral feedback this time – a statement of fact.

i) Repeat the same exercise again with change feedback this time – something you think the other person could change to improve their written work.

j) Remember to say "thank you" each time.

Exercise 3 – Non-Verbal Feedback

Go to page 13 and do **1.1f, Exercise 2 – Reading Non-Verbal Feedback while Listening.**

NOTES

Positive:

Neutral:

Change:

Intercultural Understanding

1.1b – Use intercultural understanding to interpret communication.

Mastery

You will know you are at the **Expert** level in the use of this ATL skill when you can predict accurately, accept and understand how another person's cultural background might affect their communication with you.

Intercultural understanding means appreciating that a person's upbringing and culture affects their communications with others both in terms of what they say, how they say it and what they mean.

Exercise 1 – Folk Tales

What cultural group do you identify most strongly with? Once you have decided, do the following exercise from the point of view of that cultural group – either alone or in a group of students from the same cultural group:

a) Find one common folk tale or fairy tale or nursery rhyme that is part of your culture that maybe you were told when you were young.

b) Work out what the message or meaning or moral of the story is.

c) If you are doing this in class, explain your story (briefly – maybe two minutes) to the rest of the class and tell them what the meaning or the moral of the story was.

d) Ask other cultural groups if they know of any story or fairy tale or nursery rhyme from their culture which focuses on the same message.

e) Notice if the messages, morals or meanings are different between cultures for similar stories.

f) Take one newspaper article on a current topic from a local newspaper and see if you can add to or change or re-create the newspaper article to bring out the same moral message that was in your story.

g) Describe to the rest of the class what your newspaper story looks like now.

h) Discuss how different cultural interpretations could change the emphasis in reporting in newspapers.

Exercise 2 – Social events

a) From the point of view of your chosen culture, write some key-point notes on how your culture traditionally celebrates each of the following events.

b) Describe what happens in each event and also describe what you think the most important message or theme is that is focused on by the way the event is celebrated:

 i. A family evening meal

 ii. A wedding

 iii. The birth of a child

 iv. The achievement of adulthood

 v. A successful performance – academically, in sport, music, chess, dance, etc.

c) One representative from each cultural group then needs to pin their notes on each event on one wall in your classroom under the appropriate heading.

d) Prepare a two minute presentation on one of the events and present it to the students in your class.

e) Discuss what the similarities and differences are in each event and the important moral and ethical messages that are focused on in each one.

Presentation Skills

Mastery

You will know you are at the **Expert** level in the use of this ATL skill when you are successful at connecting with any audience.

Communicating through speaking to audiences is an art which gets better with practice but it is not something that is usually spontaneous. Communicating well with any audience is a combination of good preparation and good delivery. Once you have the basics in place you will be able to communicate effectively with any audience.

Exercise 1 – Think of a presentation you have to give soon and fill in the following boxes

Describe your purpose in delivering this presentation, why are you doing it, what message do you want to get across to your audience?	My purpose is ...
Describe your audience: i. Who are they, what are their characteristics? ii. Why are they there listening to you? iii. What will they be expecting to hear?	My audience is ...
Establish your credibility, explain why you are up there delivering this presentation, what are your credentials or experience that make you the right person to be doing this?	I am ...
Tell them for how long you will be speaking and always make sure you keep track of time and Stick To Time!	I will be ...
Create an attention grabber that in some way illustrates a key point relevant to your presentation – a picture, a short video clip, a joke, a quote, a current news story, an historical reference, a story from your own life or a famous person's life, etc.	My attention grabber will be ...

Create a logical flow of idea development from beginning to end as a series of key points, each one leading to the next.	Idea 1 Idea 2 Idea 3
Use one story to illustrate each key point, a relevant example from your own life or someone else's life – current or historical.	Story to illustrate idea 1 Story to illustrate idea 2 Story to illustrate idea 3
Create a conclusion which brings the audience to the purpose of your presentation.	My conclusion is ...
Give them a task, an action to take to use your main idea.	. Action plan – what you need to do now is ...

Write up your whole presentation, not in terms of every word you are going to say but in terms of the ideas you are going to present and the stories you are going to use to illustrate each idea. Make a series of cue cards – one per idea – and number them.

Practice delivering your presentation from your cue cards, repeat until you are comfortable with it all.

delivery

Any presentation is a conversation, but instead of being a conversation between you and one person it is a conversation between you and multiple people. And it is probably a conversation in which you are going to do most of the talking but it is still a conversation. In any conversation the quality of the communication depends on both delivery and feedback. On the delivery side, there are many ways in which you can talk – authoritatively, emotionally, logically, persuasively, dogmatically, with enthusiasm and energy or without. Each style of talking sends messages to the audience that either reinforce your message or detract from your message. To deliver your message effectively you are also going to need to be very aware of response and feedback. This means that while you are speaking you need to be constantly checking to see if your message is understood, and adjusting your message based on that feedback.

Exercise 2 – Different ways of speaking

a) Take any piece of writing in your subject – a chapter in your text book or your teacher's notes – and pick a series of paragraphs that each contain several key points or facts

b) Get into pairs and work your way through the following exercises, writing down your thoughts after each one. Swap roles for each exercise.

Read different paragraphs to each other in the way described below, alternating the Reader and Listener each time and writing down what you notice each time.	**Reader** Describe how it felt to deliver the paragraph that way. What did you notice about your listener's non-verbal communication – their facial expressions, body language, eye contact?	**Listener** Describe how well you picked up the key points from the paragraph. Describe what the impact of the presentation was on you – how did you feel when listening?
Read one paragraph out loud in as boring a way as possible.		
Read another paragraph out loud as fast as possible.		
Read another paragraph out loud at conversation speed with no hand or body movement at all.		
Read another paragraph at conversation speed allowing your hands and body to move to emphasize the key points.		
Read another paragraph with great enthusiasm using big hand and body movements.		

c) Write down which delivery method worked best for you – both in terms of which was most enjoyable to deliver and which helped you understand and remember the key points best. Was it the same for both partners?

d) Did you notice any connection between eye contact and understanding?

Two key points to remember for effective presentations:

i. Motion and emotion are connected. If you want to connect with your audience's emotions, if you want them to feel a response to what you are saying, use big hand gestures and body movements to emphasize key points

ii. While you are speaking make sure you are continually moving your eyes over the audience's eyes. Any time you notice a frown or a shake of the head or any other non-verbal signal of a lack of understanding, go back over that point again, saying it in a different way.

Writing for Different Purposes

1.1d – Use appropriate forms of writing for different purposes and audiences.
1.2e – Write for different purposes.

Mastery

You will know you are at the **Expert** level in the use of this ATL skill set when you can automatically recognize and use the appropriate form of writing for different purposes and audiences.

Quality writing requires you to identify your purpose for writing and for whom you are writing – your audience. Following are different purposes for writing:

- telling a story
- writing a report
- listing instructions
- writing a poem

The different types of writing are known as **genres**. Each genre caters to a specific purpose and audience.

Following are descriptions of each genre and exercises for practicing the different writing styles.

For each exercise you can also ask for feedback. Go to page 2 and do **Exercise 1 – Verbal Feedback** for how to do that part well.

Genre	Description	Practice
Descriptive	Brings to life a person, place or thing through active, alive and rich detail; the reader is able to picture the topic in his/her mind. Used in diaries and stories.	Create a clear mental picture of a person, place or thing that you know well and then write a description using as much detail as possible.
Write 30 words about a person, place or thing: Ask someone else to read what you have written and see if they can imagine it clearly. Ask them for ways in which you could improve your descriptive writing.		
Expository	Informs and educates the reader about a topic by using facts and logical explanations. Used in reports and experiments.	Select a topic or process that you know well and write an explanation of it for someone else using facts and details.
Write 30 words to logically explain a topic: Ask someone else to imagine that they know absolutely nothing about your topic and then read what you have written. Ask them if they can follow your explanation and what they would suggest you change in order to improve it.		

Narrative	Tells a story and is often used in novels and essays in which the story moves from an introduction to climax to conclusion. Used in adventure stories and fairy tales.	Write a story about a special event you have experienced but add to it an unexpected, imaginary, dramatic conclusion.

Write 30 words about a special experience:

Ask someone else to read your story and give you feedback on how they enjoyed it and if there was anything else you could add to it to make it more interesting or exciting.

Persuasive	Used to express an opinion on a topic and to try to convert the reader to your way of thinking. Used in speeches and advertising pamphlets.	Think of a change you would love to see happen at school and write a letter to your principal to try and convince him/her to make this change happen.

Write 30 persuasive words about a topic:

Ask someone else to imagine they are the principal and get them to read your writing and tell you if they would be persuaded. Ask them for any feedback on what you could do to improve your argument.

Poetry	Used to create an emotional impact in the reader using rhyme, verse and repetition. Used in songs and poems.	Think of something from your own life that had an emotional impact on you and write something in verse that expresses how that felt. You can use rap, rhyme, rhythm or rhyming words if you want to.

Write 30 words as poem or song:

Ask someone to read your writing and give you some feedback on whether your words created an emotional impact for them. Also you could ask them to comment on any rhymes you used and if they gave the writing rhythm.

Procedure	Used to tell the reader how to make or do something through instructions. Used in recipes and instruction booklets.	Think of something that you do often and write a list of instructions that would work for someone with no knowledge at all of what you are talking about.

Write 30 words about how to do or make something:

Ask someone to imagine that they have no knowledge at all of what you are describing and ask them to read your writing and give you feedback as to whether they think they could follow your instructions. Ask them for anything they would prefer to have explained more clearly.

Multimedia Communication

Mastery

You will know you are at the **Expert** level in the use of this ATL skill when your presentations engage all audiences through multi-media approaches.

The word media can mean both the means by which you get your message across to an audience – talking, visual images, video clips, animations, PowerPoint, etc. – and the platform you use to get your message across – through a newspaper, magazine, TV, telephone, the internet, etc. Within the field of digital data transmission using the internet, there are a huge number of different "media" that can be used – messaging, face-to-face, blogs, video clips, podcasts, live feeds – as well as different systems of use – websites, social media, apps, games, etc.

The important thing to consider is choosing the most effective type of media to convey your message to the specific audience with whom you are communicating.

Exercise 1 – Media options

a. Work with a partner.

b. Imagine that you have three different types of message to get across to each of the listed audiences
  i.   an urgent message they need to get right now
  ii. a message they need to read tonight and act on tomorrow
  iii. a message that informs or educates them about something important but doesn't have any deadline for action.

c. Work through the following table and write down in each case what you think would be the best way to get the message across – see if you can come up with three or four different "media" for each one.

Audience	Message Type		
	Urgent message	**Read tonight for action tomorrow**	**Informing or educating**
Students in your class			
A friend on the other side of the world			

	Urgent message	Read tonight for action tomorrow	Informing or educating
Your teacher			
Your school principal			
Your parents			
Your grandparents			
The university you want to attend			
A prospective employer			

Exercise 2 – Media in presentations

a) For the next presentation you need to prepare for any subject, first go to page 5 and do *1.1c Exercise 1 – Designing your presentation*.

b) In your presentation, make sure you are including several different representations of information using different media and also try using different delivery platforms to get your message across.

Non-Verbal Communication

1.1f – Interpret and effectively use modes of non-verbal communication.

Mastery

You will know you are at the **Expert** level in the use of this ATL skill when you can accurately interpret and appropriately respond to all forms of non-verbal communication.

Non-verbal messages are those messages we receive all the time from another person's body language, posture and movements, their tone of voice, hand gestures, facial expressions, eye movements, etc.

Exercise 1 – Recognizing non-verbal messages

Below is a series of body language actions. Work with a partner and spend a minute or two on each body language action trying to become clear about the different message that is sent by each action. Try acting each one out, watching each other, talking through your impressions and, when you have reached agreement with each other, write down what message is being transmitted in each case:

Shrugging your shoulders	Talking with a shaky trembling voice	Sitting upright on the edge of the chair	Sitting with arms and legs crossed	Leaning back on a chair with hands on your head	Talking with your arms folded
Nodding when listening to someone	Slumping in a chair	Pacing up and down while talking	Sighing when talking to someone	Making eye contact when talking to someone	Yawning when listening to someone
Leaning forward on a chair when listening	Avoiding eye contact with someone	Smiling when someone is talking to you	Taking a deep breath when talking to someone	Leaning against a wall when talking	Fiddling with objects while talking

Write down which body language actions show people that you are interested in them and what they are saying ....

....

....

Exercise 2 – Reading non-verbal feedback while listening

a) Take any piece of writing in your subject – a chapter in your text book or your teacher's notes – and pick a series of paragraphs that each contain several key points or facts

b) Get into pairs and work your way through the following exercises, writing down your thoughts after each one. Swap roles for each exercise.

In each situation one person reads a paragraph to the other person as if they are trying to explain it to them. The listener listens in different ways each time. Read different paragraphs to each other alternating the Reader and Listener each time and writing down what you each notice each time.	**Reader** Describe how it felt to deliver the paragraph that way. What was the non-verbal message that you picked up from the listener?	**Listener** Describe what the impact of the person talking was on you – how did you feel when listening?
Reader reads, Listener listens but looks down at their desk the whole time.		
Reader reads, Listener listens and looks directly at the Reader's eyes the whole time.		
Reader reads, Listener listens but looks away, around the room, at other people the whole time.		
Reader reads, Listener listens and fiddles with things on their desk – pens, paper, etc. the whole time.		
Reader reads, Listener listens, looks at the reader from time to time and makes some notes on paper of the key points they hear.		

c) Discuss with your partner which listening method gave the Reader the feeling they were listened to most?

d) Discuss with your partner which listening method enabled the Listener to concentrate best and remember most?

e) Think about what non-verbal clues you need to anticipate when delivering a presentation, in order to gain the information you need as to whether listeners are engaged and understanding what you are saying.

Negotiation

1.1g – Negotiate ideas and knowledge with peers and teachers.

2j – Negotiate effectively.

Negotiation involves being clear about facts, opinions, and points of view and the ability to see and understand another side of any argument.

Exercise 1 – Facts and viewpoints

a) Work with someone with whom you have a disagreement that you would both like to resolve and on which you are both happy to work.

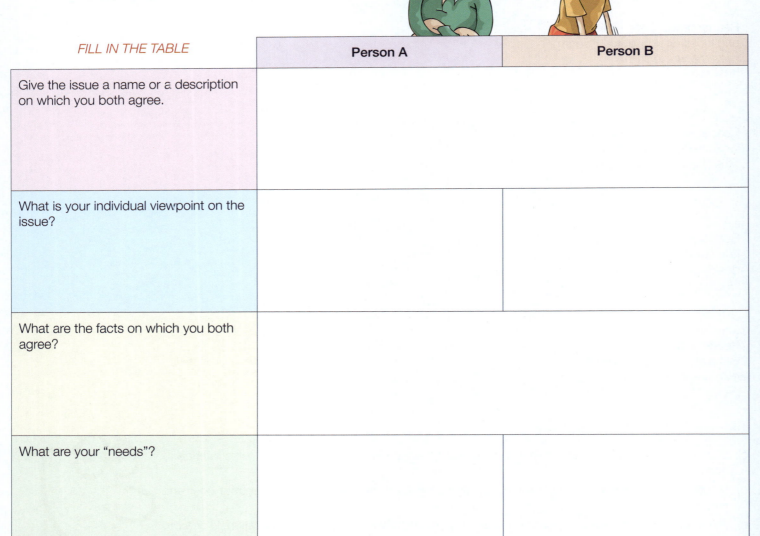

FILL IN THE TABLE	Person A	Person B
Give the issue a name or a description on which you both agree.		
What is your individual viewpoint on the issue?		
What are the facts on which you both agree?		
What are your "needs"?		

What are your "wants"?		
Restate the particular issue of contention from the other person's point of view		
Are there any aspects of this issue over which you have some flexibility of needs, wants or viewpoint?		
If anything was possible, what would be some imaginative, creative solutions to the dispute?		
If an external mediator was looking at this dispute what might be a solution they might suggest?		
Can you think of any possible solution on which you both can agree?		

c) If you did reach an agreement, what were the most useful aspects of the analysis and negotiation that helped you reach agreement?

....

....

....

....

d) If you didn't reach agreement, what would you do differently next time? How would you change the process? Draw up a new table to represent what you see as a more useful process.

Social Media

1.1h – Participate in, and contribute to, digital social media networks.
2a – Use social media networks appropriately to build and develop relationships.

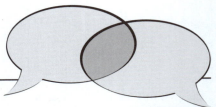

Mastery

You will know you are at the **Expert** level in the use of this ATL skill set when you are confidently using social media in a safe and appropriate way.

Feeling socially connected can be an important factor in you enjoying a healthy sense of wellbeing. Using an array of social media platforms enables you to be connected to friends, family and multiple audiences should you choose to. There are sensible and safe ways to use social media as well as other ways. You need to be aware of the best, safest and most productive ways to share all types of information with others – locally, nationally and globally.

Exercise 1 – Your connectedness...

a) Work with a partner and fill in all the boxes below, develop the answers to one table between you.

b) When you have finished, compare with another pair of students and see if they have the same answers.

c) Discuss any differences.

Questions about your life in social media.	**Answers** about your life in the digital world.
Write down all the different social media platforms, websites, apps you use at present.	
Describe the different audiences who receive your contributions to social media.	
What do you see as the main benefits of social media?	

How can social media help you to build and develop new relationships?	
What do you get (socially) from social media that you don't get in real life?	
Why do you think this is? Do you think this is problematic?	
Can you think of some ways you could get the same things from your friends in real life that you get from social media?	
What are some of the pressures and negative aspects of social media?	
What can you do to deal with the pressures and negative aspects of social media?	

Exercise 2 – Rules...

a) Work with a partner.

b) Imagine that you have been asked to give advice to a younger class at school about responsible and safe social media use.

c) First, just from your own experience, can you devise your top 5 tips that you would give to younger students.

d) Second, research the topic "rules for safe social media use" and find out what other people think.

e) Put everything you find together into a new set of top 10 rules for safe and responsible social media use.

f) Compare with another pair of students and formulate one set of 10 top rules with which you all agree.

g) Then share with another group of 4 and do it again.

h) Eventually come up with one set of rules on which the whole class agrees.

i) Write them up in a list to go on the wall of your classroom.

Digital Communication

1.1i – Collaborate with peers and experts using a variety of digital environments and media

1.1j – Share ideas with multiple audiences using a variety of digital environments and media

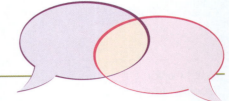

Mastery

You will know you are at the **Expert** level in the use of this ATL skill set when you can confidently share, communicate and collaborate with peers, experts and multiple audiences in the digital environment.

Working collaboratively in a group or team is an essential feature of today's schooling. The internet enables students to work in groups which mix together people from different age groups, schools, cities, cultures and countries. Although working in diverse groups is not always easy and doesn't necessarily suit every person, it is the best way to gather a wide range of experience and viewpoints on any issue and can be a very productive method of reducing the workload of individuals while still achieving group goals.

Exercise 1 – Digital collaboration

The aim of this exercise is to practice on-line collaboration in order to become clear about the strengths and weaknesses of various methods and media used and the advantages and problems of digital group work.

a) First you need a project or a problem or an area of interest you would like to investigate and a time frame and a clear outline of what you want to achieve – either from your teacher or self-generated

b) Then you need to build a group interested in working together to achieve the goals, so the first question is how will you find those people?

> The title of my project or problem to solve is: ....
> ....
> The details of the project or specification or marking criteria are: ....
> ....
> ....
> This needs to be completed by: ....
> The internet platforms I am going to use to try to find interested people are:...
> ....
> ....

c) Once you have a few people interested, you need to establish a few group norms and get everyone's agreement on them. e.g.

   i. A set time (maybe once a week) when everyone can get together using the same platform to discuss ideas

   ii. A system for sharing information with all group members outside of group meetings

   iii. A commitment to attend all meetings if possible

   iv. Timelines and deadlines for completion

   v. Rules for participation like:

   - all group members will get an opportunity to contribute at every meeting
   - all viewpoints will be listened to
   - all contributions will be valued
   - decisions will be made by consensus (see **2g,i,k – Consensus** on page 57).

d) Get each team member to indicate their strengths, what they feel they are good at – and also their areas of interest – why they are interested in this project.

e) Then it may be useful to decide on roles within the group like:
   i. Meeting organizer
   ii. Information coordinator
   iii. Researcher
   iv. Writer

f) Another way to organize the group is to divide up the whole project into specific tasks and to have each group member take one task, work on it and report back.

Once you have a functioning on-line group, the important thing to do is find the best ways that your group can support each other and share various forms of information. Add to the following table as often as possible:

	Names of websites, media, apps, etc.	Advantages and disadvantages of each
The best platforms we have found to share written information are:		
The best platforms to share digital video clips are:		
The best platforms for face-to-face communication with the whole group are:		

g) Finally, you need to consider how on-line groups are different from live groups you might set up in your classroom, and the problems, solutions, advantages and disadvantages of each.

	Advantages	Disadvantages	Problems	Solutions
Live groups				
Online groups using digital communication media				

Read Critically

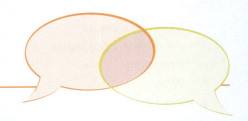

Mastery

You will know you are at the **Expert** level in the use of this ATL skill when every time you read information-based text you automatically become aware of the author's purpose, the tone and persuasive elements of the writing, and you recognize any bias.

To **non-critical** readers, texts provide facts. Readers gain knowledge by memorizing the statements within a text.

To the **critical** reader, any single text provides only one portrayal of the facts, one individual's "take" on the subject matter. Critical readers recognize not only **what** a text says, but also **how** that text portrays the subject matter. They recognize the various ways in which each and every text is the unique creation of a unique author.

Exercise 1 – Critical reading

a) Choose a piece of persuasive or factual writing – from a newspaper, magazine or textbook.

The title and author(s) are?	
When was this written and where?	
Why did the authors write this when they did?	
Your purpose or reason for reading this is?	
A question you want to answer by reading this is?	

b) First time through – before you read the text properly you need to skim read the whole piece of writing (go to page 31 and do **Exercise 1 – Skim Reading** first to learn how to skim read) and become clear about the organization and structure of development of the ideas in the text

c) Second time through – read the text thoroughly now and write down each key idea as you come to it

d) For each idea, look for and note down briefly what the nature of the supporting arguments are and your own reactions to each one – both emotional reactions (you don't believe it, you love it, etc.) and any questions that occur to you. Try to do all this as you read. The more you practice it the better you will get at doing it all automatically.

Sequence of ideas developed in order	How the author supports each idea			My reactions	
	Facts	Opinions	Speculation and conjectures	Emotional reactions	Question I have
Idea 1 ...					
Idea 2 ...					
Idea 3 ...					
Idea 4 ...					
Idea 5 ...					

e) Once you have finished, look back over your summary and create an analysis of the text making sure you include:

    i.   A summary of the key ideas in sequence, written in your own words, as you understand them

    ii.   The strength and weaknesses of the authors facts and arguments

    iii.   Any bias you have picked up

    iv.   The author's overall viewpoint and if that is the same as or different from other authors on the topic

    v.   The validity of the author's sources, references, quotes.

f) Write a paragraph in your own words of any new understandings you have gained from the text:

    i.   what are the new things you have learned?

    ii.   how or where can you use what you have learned?

Read for Variety

1.2b – Read a variety of sources for information and for pleasure.

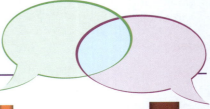

Mastery

You will know you are at the **Expert** level in the use of this ATL skill when you regularly read from a variety of sources and you know where to go, to find written information on a variety of topics.

Exercise 1 – Logging sources

a) Written information is provided to you in many different ways. Try to keep a log of all the sources of written information that you use in one week

b) Put a check in the correct box each time you read something from one of these sources:

Fiction book.. ☐	Other mail received................................. ☐
Non-fiction book.................................. ☐	Library catalogue .... ☐
Comic book... ☐	Search engine .... ☐
Magazine.. ☐	School subject website.......................... ☐
Published journal or periodical .... ☐	Blog .... ☐
Your own journal or diary .... ☐	Other website.. ☐
Musical score .... ☐	Text message .... ☐
Calendar... ☐	Chat message .... ☐
Script for a play or production .... ☐	Other social media message.................. ☐
Advertising billboard .... ☐	Other written words............................... ☐
Graffiti.. ☐	.... ☐
Restaurant menu................................. ☐	.... ☐
Bank statement, bill............................. ☐	

c) See how many different sources you can find for the same information:

Think of something that fits the following description and see in how many different places you can find something written about it or them.	My subject was:	The places I found something written about it or them were:
A famous sports person		
A famous musician		
A famous artist		
An important person in history		
A current world leader		
Your country		
Your school		
Your city		
The street you live on		
Today's weather		
Today's TV programs		
Make up your own subject...		
1.		
2.		
3.		
4.		

Inferences & Conclusions

1.2c – Make inferences and draw conclusions.

Difference between Imply and Infer:

Someone who gives information may imply something in what they say, someone who receives information may infer something from information they receive.

- Implications are unstated possibilities raised from the analysis of available information which are suggested but not specified.
- Inferences are guesses made based on available information and clues picked up that are open to be verified or proven to be wrong based on subsequent information.
- Conclusions are decisions based on facts.

Exercise 1 – Practice drawing inferences

a) Work in pairs.

b) Each find one fiction book that one person is familiar with that the other person hasn't read yet.

c) The person who hasn't read the book then takes sticky notes and randomly marks four pages – one near the beginning of the book, one in the middle, one three quarters of the way through and one near or at the end of the story.

d) Next they open the page to the first mark and read one or two paragraphs only on the page they have marked.

e) Do the same for the next three marked pages – reading only one paragraph per page.

f) When they finish they need to write down or describe all the inferences they can draw:

    a. about the plot of the story – what do they think happens in the story – at the beginning, in the middle and at the end?

    b. about the characters in the story – how many characters have they identified, what are their names, who are they, how old are they, what do they each do in the story?

g) The person who has read the book before then tells them how close to the actual story they got and if they identified some of the characters correctly.

h) Both people now swap roles and do the same exercise again with a different book.

i) Discuss what sort of information gives you the most useful clues to help draw accurate conclusions.

Exercise 2 – Practice drawing accurate inferences

a) Find some short (1-3 minute) news reports, political speeches and advertisements (preferably from another country that you are not familiar with) on any website.

b) Try watching just one quarter of each clip and write down anything that was stated as a fact.

c) Then by yourself or with a partner try to work out what you think the conclusion will be.

d) Then watch the clip to the end and see how accurately you predicted the end.

Facts	Inferences	Were you correct?
What was stated as true so far?	What do you think the conclusion will be?	

e) Which ones were easiest to predict the end?

f) Why was that?

Exercise 3 – 20 questions

a) Work in pairs.

b) One person thinks of one particular aspect or object or example from within a certain topic that you have both just finished working on and the other person has to guess what is being thought of by asking questions.

c) But all the questions have to be questions that only require a Yes or No answer. No other questions are allowed.

d) Swap roles and do it again.

Exercise 4 – Practice drawing conclusions

a) Work in pairs both with the same subject text book.

b) Each person turns to a section or a topic in the textbook that neither of them has covered yet – a different one each – and reads one section.

c) Each person then writes down four facts from the topic they were reading that lead to a particular conclusion – but don't write down the conclusion.

d) Swap pieces of paper and try to work out what the conclusion will be given the facts in front of you.

e) Swap pieces of paper again and discuss how accurately you have drawn each conclusion.

f) Discuss what sort of information made it easiest to draw a conclusion accurately.

g) Do the exercise again, with different topics and try to focus on writing the four facts in a sequence that will help the other person to draw the correct conclusion.

25

Exercise 5 – Use available information to draw conclusions

a) Work in pairs.

b) Read the following passage together and then answer all the questions as best you can. If you can't use the information given to draw conclusions then just guess. But make your best guess based on what you know. Separate out the conclusions from the guesses in the table below:

> Henry woke up, rolled over carefully and eased out from under the duvet. He noticed that the bruising on his shins was much reduced and he thought he might still be OK for Saturday. He went carefully down the wooden stairs and noticed a pleasing aroma in the air. The table was set with warm apple muffins and brewed coffee. A note was left on the table. It said "bacon and hash browns in the oven, good luck at the doctor's, just rest up, you deserve it S.H.". Next to the note was a wrapped present with a bow on top.

Question	Conclusion	Best Guess
Who was Henry?		
Where was he staying?		
What had caused the bruising?		
What was going to happen on Saturday?		
What was the aroma?		
Who was S.H.?		
Why was Henry going to the doctor's?		
Why might he need some good luck?		
Why did Henry need to rest up?		
Who was to receive the present?		
What was the reason for the present?		
What was in the present?		

Symbols

1.2d – Use and interpret a range of discipline-specific terms and symbols.

1.2f – Understand and use mathematical notation.

Mastery

You will know you are at the **Expert** level in the use of this ATL skill set when you can recall and describe what all the terms and symbols in this subject mean and how you use them – accurately and in your mother-tongue.

Understanding terms and symbols in every subject means being able to describe what they mean, and how to use them accurately and in your own words so they have meaning for you.

Exercise 1 – Understanding terms and symbols

a) Find all the important terms and symbols in your subject (often found in a glossary, near the front or in the back of your textbook), choose some that you don't really understand yet and write them into this table.

b) Find the definition as it is written in the textbook and copy that in the next column.

c) Using your mother-tongue, in your own words, write in a description of what that symbol or term means and how you can use it within this subject.

If you have trouble doing this stage, find a senior student or a teacher who has the same mother-tongue as you and ask them to explain it to you.

Persist until you have a clear understanding of every one – this will help greatly in your understanding of every subject.

Subject-specific terms and symbols	Definition	What that means to you – in your own language	
		Describe in your own words what this term or symbol means	Describe in your own words how you can use this term or symbol

Exercise 2 – Using symbols and terms

a) From your list of subject-specific terms and symbols, pick four and copy out one example from the textbook of the correct use of each term or symbol.

b) Make up your own example of using each term or symbol in a similar way to a).

c) Make up a third example of the use of each one using the same symbol or term in a completely different way.

d) Ask another student or the teacher to check you have understood and used each symbol or term correctly.

e) If you have not used it correctly yet, find a senior student or a teacher who has the same mother-tongue as you and ask them to explain it to you in language you understand well.

f) Go back to Exercise 1 and change your description in your own language where necessary.

Term or Symbol	One example of use from the textbook	Own example of use	Different example of use

Paraphrase

1.2g – Paraphrase accurately and concisely.

Mastery

You will know you are at the **Expert** level in the use of this ATL skill when you can create a summary of key points from spoken or written words that represents an accurate reflection of the work.

Paraphrasing is all about listening well or reading for understanding, and being able to write key-points in summary form at the same time. It takes practice to become proficient at this but it is probably the most important skill for university.

First you need to work through the two note-making exercises on page 33:

1.2i – Take effective notes in class
1.2j – Make effective notes for studying

Exercise 1 – Listening and paraphrasing

a) Get into groups of 3.

b) Each person first needs to think of a topic on which they could speak for two minutes – any topic at all – something you are interested in, an experience you have had or a special holiday you have taken.

c) In the Speaker Thoughts section each person needs to write down 10 key points they are going to describe.

SPEAKER THOUGHTS What are your thoughts on the idea? You have to speak for two minutes.

---

d) Next decide who will be the first Speaker, Listener and Scribe. You will all get to take each role so it doesn't matter who is in which role to begin with.

e) The first Speaker speaks for two minutes (timed) on their topic, the listener listens and the Scribe writes down key points.

LISTENER Listen carefully with full attention and try to imagine exactly what the speaker is describing so that you can paraphrase back to the Speaker what you think s/he has said.

SCRIBE NOTES Record what the Speaker and Listener have said and what their intentions were.

_____

f) When the speaker has finished speaking, the listener paraphrases back to them the key points of what they said as accurately as possible.

g) The Scribe then adds any points the Listener missed that they noticed and wrote down.

h) The Speaker then confirms how accurately they have been listened to and adds any additional things that were missed.

i) Discuss what are the important things on which to focus when listening actively.

IMPORTANT THINGS TO FOCUS ON WHEN LISTENING AND PARAPHRASING

_____

j) Change roles and do the exercise again.

k) Change roles and do the exercise for the third and last time.

l) Discuss what you have learned about listening and paraphrasing.

Skim Reading

1.2h – Preview and skim texts to build understanding.

Mastery

You will know you are at the **Expert** level in the use of this ATL skill when you can process a chapter of any textbook in just a few minutes and get from it a summary of the key points of information that you need.

Learning to skim-read is a vital skill for effective learning, especially if you are thinking of going on to university where the quantity of information you will be required to process in most degrees is so large that there is no way you will be able to read all of it at normal reading speed. If you have learned how to skim-read or speed-read you can cut down the time required for this reading enormously.

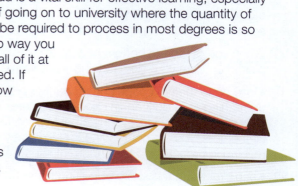

There are many levels of proficiency in skim-reading and speed-reading. It is a skill that everyone can learn and although it does take significant practice to become very good at it, everyone can learn how to increase their information processing speed with just a few simple exercises.

Exercise 1 – Newspapers and magazines

a) Find a magazine or newspaper article on something in which you are interested – one in which the article is written in columns rather than in pages.

b) On a clean page, write at the top why you are reading it, what interests you about this article and what would you like to find out more about.

c) Put your finger at the top of the first page in the middle of the first column and focus your eyes just above your finger. Run your finger and your eyes down the center of the first column, faster than you could possibly read it but slow enough to be able to see the words you are looking at. Do not try to read the words just look at the words but keep your eyes focused only on the center of the column of writing.

d) When you get to the bottom stop, and try writing down on your page anything that you picked up from your skim reading – any words, ideas, facts, figures, etc.

e) Move onto the next column and repeat the process. If you are picking up nothing at all do it again slower, if you are picking up too much do it again faster. Find your own best speed for skimming. Remember, you are not reading for pleasure you are reading in order to find the information that will answer the question you wrote at the top of the page. You might want to substitute a pen or pencil for your finger.

f) Keep practicing this exercise getting faster and faster until you can skim read whole columns in a few seconds and get out the essential facts.

g) Once you feel comfortable with this skill, try using the same technique to skim read a chapter of a text book – one column at a time or one page at a time.

Exercise 2 – Reading fiction fast ... find a fiction book that you are interested in reading and use that to practice the next technique

a) Turn to a chapter you haven't read yet. Using a pencil draw two vertical lines down each page in the chapter. One vertical line will be one third of the page in from the left side of the page, the other vertical line will be one third of the page in from the right side of the page, effectively dividing the text on each page into three columns.

b) This time try 'reading' the information line by line but by only looking at two points on each line – where the vertical pencil mark intersects the written text line. Using the tip of a pencil or the tip of a finger to focus your eyes, look first at where the first vertical pencil line intersects the first line of text then where the second vertical pencil line intersects the first line of text, then look where the first vertical line intersects the second line of text then where the second vertical line crosses the second line of text, etc., etc., all the way down the page line by line. You are not trying to read the text you are just trying to look at only two points on each line and trusting in your brain's ability to read by looking. The idea is to build up a smooth rhythm of eye movements.

c) When you get to the bottom of a page stop, and try writing down anything that you picked up from your skim reading – any words, ideas, facts, figures, etc.

d) Move on to the next page and repeat the process. If you are picking up nothing at all do it again slower. If you are picking up too much do it again faster. Find your own best speed for skimming. Remember, you are not reading for pleasure you are reading in order to find the important information.

e) Keep practicing this exercise getting faster and faster until you can skim read whole pages in a few seconds and get out all the essential information.

f) Once you feel comfortable with this skill try using the same technique to skim read a chapter of a novel that you have to read for school.

Exercise 3 – Speed reading textbooks for effective information extraction

a) **Goal** – decide how many pages of the textbook to process in one sitting – set a realistic goal.

b) **Review** – recall what you already know about the subject.

c) **Question** – what is your reason for reading it? Create a question to be answered and write it at the top of a new page.

d) **Skim** – first glance at every page, sweep eyes from top to bottom – (1st time through).

e) On a clean page start your summary using your chosen method (see page 33 – *1.2j – Make effective notes for studying*), by writing in the main topic.

f) **Scan** – next, go back to the beginning of the information and look through again – this time only reading the pictures, graphs, tables, illustrations and their captions (2nd time through).

g) Now add all the main headings to your summary.

h) **Look** – read the first and final sentences of each paragraph with full comprehension and speed-read the rest, using a pen to focus your eyes (3rd time through) – highlight any particularly significant words.

i) Add all the main ideas to your summary.

j) **Read** – go back and thoroughly read only that information which contains the answer to your first question.

k) Finish off your summary by adding all the important keywords.

l) When the summary is finished, close the textbook and explain your summary to yourself in your own words. If there are any parts you cannot explain, go back to the text and find new words to add to your summary so that it makes sense to you. Explain that part to yourself again.

Summary

Note-making

Mastery

You will know you are at the **Expert** level in the use of this ATL skill set when you can record the most significant information from a textbook or from a presentation (teacher talking, video, podcast) in summary form with enough detail to be able to clearly and accurately explain the ideas and concepts in your own words.

> Note-making for Understanding: The essence of developing understanding and remembering well is being able to *explain things in your own words*.

There are three parts to the development of these two skills:
- First you have to learn how to accurately identify key words, concepts and ideas in written and spoken text
- Second you have to learn how to create written summaries several different ways
- Third, you have to practice turning your own summaries back into sentences, in your own words.

Exercise 1 – Summarizing written text from a text book or from teachers' notes ... what works for you?

a) Take a series of four topics from the textbook or from teachers' notes in any subject – with about a half a page of writing per topic.

b) Read through each topic and in every sentence, highlight the most important words – keywords, ideas, concepts – aim to only highlight 2-4 words per sentence

c) Now write your own notes for each topic using the words you have highlighted and write each topic using a different note-making method as below:

   i) **Idea mapping** – write the first topic in the centre of a clean page (landscape) then add to it all the main headings as branches out from the centre. Out of the keywords in the text that you have highlighted find the main ideas and attach them to the headings as branches. Finally attach all the remaining highlighted words to the ideas as branches.

   ii) **Linear notes** – looking at your second topic, create a note summary in the form of:

   Topic

   Heading 1
   - Idea 1   - keywords ...
   - Idea 2   - keywords ...
   - Idea 3   - keywords ...

   Heading 2
   - Idea 4   - keywords ...
   - Idea 5, etc.

   iii) **Visual note-making** – with your third topic, look at the development of the ideas through the topic and create a flowchart which shows the progression of the ideas:

⇨	⇨	⇨	

In each box either write the keypoint using your highlighted headings, ideas and keywords or draw small pictures to represent the same or use a combination of words and pictures.

iv) **Vertical notes**

     a. take a clean page and draw a vertical line down your page about 1/3 of the way across the page from the left side (for right handed people), or from the right side (for left handed people).

     b. write the most important information on your page ONLY ON THE 2/3 SIDE OF THE PAGE. Make sure you write down all the facts correctly but write them in a way that makes sense to you.

     c. when the presentation has finished, read through what you have written and make a summary of key points in the 1/3 column on your page.

d) Work with a partner. You will first be looking at your Idea-map summary, they will be looking at the original text in the text book or the teachers' notes. Try to explain, as fully as you can, the meaning of all the key points you have written down on your mind-map, IN YOUR OWN WORDS. When you have finished, ask for feedback from your partner as to whether they understood your explanation and if your explanation covered all the most important material in the topic accurately.

e) Using the feedback from your partner as a guide, go back to your idea-map summary and the original notes and add in enough extra information to enable you to understand the points on which you were not clear. Explain those points to your partner again. Notice the type of words you need to highlight and on which you need to focus to enable you to explain your summaries to your partner in your own words:

The type of words I need to focus on highlighting are ....

....

f) Repeat parts c & d for all the other three summary note-making methods and, when you have finished, decide which method seems to work best for you.

g) Practice using that note-making method until you have mastered it.

Exercise 2 – Summarizing spoken words from a teacher, a video or a podcast

When your teacher is talking to you in class and writing notes on the board, the best thing you can do to develop understanding and good memory for all the information is not to write down every word you hear and see, but to write down all the facts accurately and connect them together in a way that works well for you.

a) Before you start writing your notes you need to make sure you have several different colored ballpoint pens available or one pen with several colors inside

b) Get very clear about the purpose of the presentation, video, podcast. Why are you doing this, what is the learning objective, what do you need to understand? Write the purpose at the top of the page, as a question to answer – What I need to understand is ....

c) Actively listen to the presentation and write the most important information on your page using your preferred summary note-making method from Exercise 1. Make sure you write down all the facts correctly but write them in a way that makes sense to you.

d) Listen for ideas and when the presenter changes to a new idea change to a different color. This way your notes will look more interesting, each idea will be separated from every other idea by being in a different color, you will be less likely to get distracted and you will focus more on listening for ideas

e) Now check for understanding by working with a partner again who has just done the same note-making exercise. You both need to look at your summary of key points and explain, as fully as you can, the meaning of all the key points you have written down, IN YOUR OWN WORDS. When you have finished, ask your partner if they understood your explanation, if it covered all the most important material from the presentation accurately and if they can add in any points that you missed.

f) Using the feedback from your partner as a guide, go back to your summary notes and add in enough extra information to enable you to understand the points you weren't clear on.

g) Explain those points to your partner again.

Exercise 3 – Make effective notes for studying

For this exercise I am going to introduce you to using a THOrTmap approach to note-making for study.

A THOrTmap is a type of idea map which has been developed specifically for use as a summary tool for preparation for exams.

Try it and see if it works well for you.

A THOrTmap looks like this:

THOrTmap *Topic – Headings – ideas in Order – Triggerwords*

The structure of a THOrTmap starts with the main **Topic** in the middle of the page, with a layer of **Headings** branching out from there, we then put all the **Ideas in Order** branching out from each **Heading** and lastly we add in the **Triggerwords** (also known as key-words) as branches from the **Ideas**. The first letters of those words spell out the made up word **THOrT**.

The important things to notice about **THOrTmaps** are:

- make sure you have no more than 5 branches at any point on the THOrTmap – to help with the movement of information into long-term memory

- information is linked from the 'big picture' down to the detail in the same way your brain stores information

- you can add color, small pictures, diagrams to the THOrTmap to make it appeal to all parts of your brain and all ways of thinking

Using a THOrTmap to make summary notes for studying for exams.

1. Decide how many pages of notes you want to summarise in one session.

2. Skim read every page – using a guide (a pen or pencil) to keep your eyes focused on the page, pass your eyes quickly over every word on each page – don't try and read the words just make sure you look at every word on every page – only spend about 5-10 seconds looking at each page.

3. Write the first main **TOPIC** in the middle of a clean page (turn the page sideways – landscape). Add to it all the **HEADINGS**, as branches – a maximum of 5 Headings per **THOrTmap**. If you have more than 5 Headings you will need to make a second **THOrTmap**.

4. Back to the first page of the notes you are summarizing: now, actively read the material at your normal reading speed and search for the **TRIGGERWORDS** – highlight them. The **TRIGGERWORDS** are the most important words in any sentence – the key words. Try to only highlight one or two **TRIGGERWORDS** per sentence.

5. Transfer all the **TRIGGERWORDS** onto your THOrTmap. Group the **TRIGGERWORDS** around key **IDEAs** and attach the Ideas to the Headings **in Order**.

6. When you have finished making your **THOrTmap**, highlight different sections in different colors, add in small pictures, diagrams, cartoons to maximize the sensory connections your brain makes with the information – words and images.

7. Pick up your completed **THOrTmap** and, out loud, turn your **THOrTmap** back into sentences. Explain it to yourself, out loud, in your own words.

8. For any parts you don't yet understand, go back to the original book or notes and pull out a few more words to add to your **THOrTmap**. Explain that part to yourself again.

9. Take a 10-minute break, then come back, look at your **THOrTmap** again and, out loud once again, turn your **THOrTmap** back into sentences. Explain it to yourself again, in your own words.

10. In the next 24 hours, take your **THOrTmap** out again and explain the whole thing to yourself once more, putting it back into sentences, in your own words.

11. One week after you made the **THOrtmap** review it by repeating Step 10.

12. One month after you made the **THOrTmap** review it by repeating Step 10 once more.

13. By now all the information will be in long-term memory.

14. Test yourself by finding an old exam question on the topic you been studying and write an answer to the question without referring back to your notes. Check your answer with your notes.

Writing Organizers

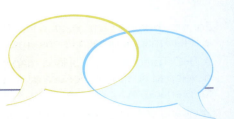

1.2k – Use a variety of organizers for academic writing tasks.

Mastery

You will know you are at the **Expert** level in the use of this ATL skill when you can confidently identify and use the most appropriate organizer for all pieces of writing you are asked to complete.

Organizers are useful tools to help you organize your writing. Some are graphic organizers which give you a visual template to follow; some are more descriptive. Organizers are planning tools which have been developed by experts in the field to give you a pattern or structure that you can follow. If you have difficulty with any writing tasks, graphic organizers can be a great help in improving your writing.

Quality pieces of writing logically and smoothly flow from thought to thought for all genres, including descriptive, expository, narrative, persuasive, poetry and procedure writing.

Exercise 1 – Finding writing organizers

a) Work with a partner.
b) Research the topic "organizers for writing tasks" and see if you can find one or two good organizers for each of the different genres of writing.
c) Describe or draw each organizer in the spaces provided – make sure you include the URL or website address where you found it.

WRITING GENRE	ORGANIZER
Descriptive. Brings to life a person, place or thing through active, alive and rich detail; the reader is able to picture the topic in his/her mind. Used in diaries and stories.	Reference:
Expository. Informs and educates the reader about a topic by using facts and logical explanations. Used in reports and experiments.	Reference:
Narrative. Tells a story and is often used in novels and essays in which the story moves from an introduction to climax to conclusion. Used in adventure stories and fairy tales.	Reference:

Persuasive. Used to express an opinion on a topic and to try to convert the reader to your way of thinking. Used in speeches and advertising pamphlets.	Reference:
Poetry. Used to tell a story to the reader using rhyme, verse and repetition. Used in songs and poems.	Reference:
Procedure. Used to tell the reader how to make or do something through instructions. Used in recipes and instruction booklets.	Reference:

Exercise 2 – Using T.E.E.L. ... a paragraph organizer

The next time you have an essay to write, of any type

a) Use the appropriate organizer that you found in Exercise 1 to organize the overall structure of your writing

b) Try using the following paragraph organizer (called TEEL) to organize each paragraph.

T.E.E.L. stands for:

Title sentence –   the first sentence explains what the paragraph will be about; not too long

Explanation –   expand on the Title sentence to discuss your thoughts about it; your reasons and arguments

Evidence –   provide support for your thoughts, reasons and arguments; for an argumentative essay your supporting evidence would be trends and statistics, and for a book your supporting evidence would be quotes from and references to the book

Link –   one or two sentences that conclude with the main point and link back to the Title sentence

c) Did using the organizers help you write the essay?

d) Was there anything that didn't help?

What worked for me was ....
....
....

What didn't work for me was ....
....
....

Report Writing

1.2n – Structure information in summaries, essays and reports.

Mastery

You will know you are at the **Expert** level in the use of this ATL skill when you can confidently create summaries, essays and reports in any subject.

All essays have a similar structure – which can be simply thought of as Introduction, Discussion and Conclusion – but there are many structures you can use to write the perfect essay.

Exercise 1 – Making summaries

a) For structuring information into summaries see **1.2j – Make effective notes for studying, Excercise 3** on page 35.

Exercise 2 – Writing essays

When you write your next essay in any of your school subjects, make sure you go through each of the following steps:

a) Get organized – get all the marking criteria from the teacher and make sure you understand exactly what is expected of you, what topics will be acceptable, how many words are required – maximum and minimum – for what will marks or grades be given, what is the deadline, how serious is the deadline?

b) Pick a topic – you might be able to choose some aspect or idea in which you are interested in or you might be given a topic.

c) Turn the topic into a question, the answer to which will meet all the criteria of the task given to you by the teacher.

d) Find key words – first go to a very general reference source, e.g. Wikipedia, and look up your topic. Use that first source simply to gather a collection of key words that relate to your topic – the relevant areas that you could talk about in your essay.

e) Use the key words to make a rough plan of what aspects of the topic you are going to describe or discuss and in what order.

f) Research – use search tools (see **6a Exercise 3** on page 127) and your key words to find useful information (avoid Wikipedia from now on) on each aspect of your essay. Each time you find something you think might be useful, write down or save the full reference. Focus on collecting information and sources at this stage rather than reading too thoroughly, just skim read (see **1.2h Exercise 1** on page 31) each source you find. Make sure also you find examples of other essays on the same or similar topics and save for looking at later.

g) Read – put aside time to read through all your researched material. Focus on your initial question – each time you come to something that you think might be of use in your essay, either copy by hand or use cut-and-paste to build up a file of quotes, ideas and examples relevant to your essay.

h) Plan – decide on the structure of the essay, e.g. one common structure is the 5 paragraph essay:

Paragraph 1. Introduction: sets the tone, grabs the attention – an anecdote, quote, historical or modern reference, headline; and develops the thesis which includes both the topic and the point, purpose or perspective of the essay – as a statement not a question or an opinion.

    i. Brainstorm: use your thesis as the prompt and write down anything that comes to mind in terms of related topics – ask who, what, when, where, why, how?

    ii. Topic sentences: use the brainstorm as the basis of creating three or more topic sentences that can be expanded to form the body of the essay.

Paragraphs 2-4. Arguments: usually the strongest first – including evidence for and against and a coherent argument that supports the direction of the essay. Include at least one quote and one reference for each argument. Avoid "I" statements and opinion.

Paragraph 5. Conclusion: pulls all the arguments together into one overarching statement or one unique perspective which either supports or disproves the thesis and may suggest implications or make predictions for future action.

RESEARCH

i) Whatever the structure you choose, write in draft form first, not worrying too much about coherence, spelling or grammar but making sure you reference well as you write – use in-text citations connected to full, written references or URLs.

j) Start writing. Look at all the cut-and-paste material you have accumulated and organize it into a coherent flow. Rewrite each piece in your own words and connect all the pieces together using your own sentences. Keep track of your references.

k) Once you have it all drafted out, look over the work as a whole and look at the development of the ideas in the essay – do they flow logically and smoothly from beginning to end, does it create reader interest, is it enjoyable to read? Adjust your essay plan and your writing to suit.

CONCLUSIONS

l) If you have time, either get someone to read your essay to you out loud or record yourself saying it and play it back. Focus on the flow and sequence of ideas and the connections between them. Make changes where necessary.

m) Write the final copy, all text, all references, check all spelling, punctuation and grammar.

n) Leave it for a day or so, go back to it and do a final check. Thin out any overused words, any repetition, any unnecessary inflation or exaggeration of material.

o) Hand it in – preferably one day before it's due.

Exercise 3 – Writing scientific reports

When writing scientific reports make sure you include all of the following:

a) Summary – this is the first paragraph in a scientific report that gives the reader a short summary of the investigation and the conclusion (it is usually best to write this last even though it comes first in your report).

EXPERIMENT

b) Topic and research – what your general topic is and why it caught your interest. What the specific focus of your research is and what you discovered.

c) Research question – what was the question you were trying to answer with your investigation?

d) Experiment – describe your experiment – the aim, the equipment, all the steps in the procedure you used, any modifications you made to your procedure as you went along.

e) Results – what actually happened when you ran your experiment, all your observations and all the data you collected.

f) Analysis and discussion – tables, graphs, statistical analysis of your data, any patterns you noticed or any correlations or trends you found that helped you make predictions, (see **8d Interpret Data** on page 165 for how to do this).

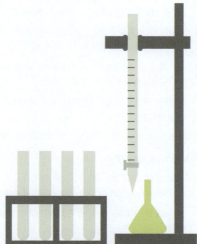

g) Conclusions – did the results of your experiment answer your research question? If not why not? What did you learn from this?

h) Comments – if you conducted this investigation again what changes would you make to the experiment or the procedure? Have the results shown you any other area you would like to research further?

i) References – make sure you cite properly all the books, papers, journals, websites and people who helped you.

Exercise 4 – Writing business reports

When writing business reports make sure you include all of the following:

a) Cover letter or memorandum – usually reports are written at the request of someone else. The cover letter or memorandum is just a couple of paragraphs which:

   i. describe the purpose of the report, the request that the report is satisfying

   ii. acknowledge any assistance in its preparation

   iii. indicate actions proposed.

b) Title page – this is a brief description of the project, including date of submission, authors, affiliations, etc.

c) Executive summary – no longer than one page, clear description of purpose, research, conclusions and key recommendations.

d) Table of contents – all headings and page numbers.

e) Introduction – a description of the context of the report, what brought it about, its purpose, the issue or problem to be explored, the scope, the structure of the report, any limitations and, finally, an expectation of the final result.

f) Findings and discussion – this is the main body of the report, information provided, evidence analyzed, arguments constructed, cost/benefit ratios calculated.

g) Conclusions – drawing meaning and significance from the findings, creating inferences based on evidence and reasoning.

h) Recommendations – drawing logical consequences from the conclusions to suggest future action, making predictions, determining probability, narrowing the range down to one or two recommendations.

i) References – in-text citations need to be referenced clearly in a bibliography, using the system in place in your school.

j) Appendices – supplementary material that provides more detail around key points.

Exercise 5 – Writing Email Reports

When writing emails as a part of schoolwork or when you are in paid employment, use the following suggestions to make your email messages as clear and as effective as possible:

When writing:

a) Keep it short, one or two issues, separated by white space.

b) Make the subject line something the reader can use as a reference for the contents.

c) All e-mail is public, don't ever send anything you wouldn't want the whole world to see.

d) Watch your tone, avoid jokes, puns, irony, especially when dealing with people from different cultures.

e) Adopt a straight-forward factual manner and make sure every point is clear, using repetition where necessary.

f) Make sure your signature doesn't dominate the look of the email – be subtle with your signature.

g) Recheck everything, including attachments before you hit Send.

When responding:

h) Answer within 24 hours even if it is just to say *"Got your message, will send you a more detailed answer as soon as I can."*

i) Read the message to which you are responding very carefully – answer each point in turn.

j) Be careful with *cc'd* and *Reply All*, only include people who need the information – don't be responsible for filling up other people's in-boxes needlessly.

k) Cut the tail off the mail – send only the last couple of messages, not the whole history every time.

Self-Assessment of ATL Skills

To see how best to use this page refer to pages 114 and 115.

ATL Skills	Novice *Watch*	Learner *Copy*	Practitioner *Do*				Expert *Share*
			Starting	*Practicing*	*Getting better*	*Got it!*	
Feedback							
Intercultural Understanding							
Presentation Skills							
Writing for Different Purposes							
Multimedia Communication							
Non-Verbal Communication							
Negotiation							
Social Media							
Digital Communication							
Read Critically							
Read for Variety							
Inferences & Conclusions							
Symbols							
Paraphrase							
Skim Reading							
Note-making							
Writing Organizers							
Report Writing							

Table title: **Student Self-Assessment of ATL Skills Proficiency – COMMUNICATION SKILLS**

Notes

COLLABORATION SKILLS

To collaborate means to work together cooperatively with others to achieve common goals. Collaboration can occur between individuals, between organizations, businesses, political parties, governments, etc., but it always means people communicating with other people and being prepared to listen, to consider other people's points of view and to work to come to decisions on which parties agree. Collaboration is the essence of teamwork where the resources of a group of people are combined to achieve more than each individual could achieve alone.

Through practicing the skills in this cluster, you will get better at both effective group processes like listening well, understanding others, negotiating, delegating, building consensus, making fair decisions; and the individual skills you need to advocate for your own rights, deal well with feedback, take responsibility for your own actions and lead others.

The skills in this cluster are the skills you will need to get any group work or team work project in which you are involved to work well for every member of the group.

GREAT COLLABORATIONS

Germany invaded Poland on September 1, 1939. Because Great Britain had pledged military support to Poland if it were attacked by the Germans, it subsequently declared war against Germany on September 3, 1939, beginning World War II.

The second World War initially did not go well for Great Britain and by April 1941 Germany occupied and controlled most of Europe. Germany was not able to successfully invade Great Britain, however, and in June 1941 turned to the East and invaded Russia. This invasion forced Joseph Stalin (the leader of the Soviet Union) to seek military help. Despite the very different political systems in Russia, the United States and Great Britain, the threat of a common enemy brought the Allies together into a great collaboration.

Through discussions in Casablanca (1941), Tehran (1943 and Yalta (1945), Winston Churchill (Prime Minister of Great Britain), Franklin D. Roosevelt (President of the US) and Joseph Stalin (General Secretary of the Soviet Union's Communist Party) formed one of the greatest ever collaborations to fight against their common enemy, Nazi Germany.

By 1945 at a cost of 26,000,000 Russians, 3,500,000 people of the British Commonwealth and 400,000 US troops, the collaborative alliance known as the "Allies" had defeated Nazi Germany.

This was probably the single greatest collaboration of different thinking people that most shaped the world as we know it today.

Empathy

Mastery

You will know you are at the **Expert** level in the use of this ATL skill when you can recognize feelings expressed by other people and also understand and accept another person's point of view.

Showing empathy for the point of view and the needs and feelings of others, and communicating that you understand and accept these things, creates social connectedness, which is an important component in effective communication and collaboration.

EXERCISE 1 – Walk a mile in my shoes #1

a) Work with a partner.

b) Find an article or editorial from a newspaper, magazine or journal, or a topic from your textbook or teachers' notes in any subject that considers two opposing points of view.

c) Take one side of the argument and do a little more research and write down the key points of that side of the argument. Read it over until you can hold that opinion and argue your case only from that point of view.

d) Set up a discussion with your partner where you each take the point of view you have read about and argue your case from that point of view. Make sure you both get a chance to state your case – one person talks and the other listens then change. Keep going until you both have finished your side of the argument.

e) Did anyone clearly win the argument?

f) Now swap roles and swap notes.

g) Read the other person's notes and consider their point of view.

h) Discuss the issue again but this time make your argument from the opposing point of view.

i) Does the same side of the argument win?

j) Think about whether you were able to understand the argument from both sides.

k) Did you notice that you felt differently when arguing the two sides?

EXERCISE 2 – Walk a mile in my shoes #2

First you need to have completed *ATL skill 8.b Gather and organize relevant information to formulate an argument* on page 161 in order to construct your own argument by looking at the evidence for both sides.

a) Work with a partner.

b) Take one side each of the argument you have constructed.

c) Do a little more research if necessary and write down the key points of that side of the argument. Read it over until you can hold that opinion and argue your case only from that point of view.

d) Set up a discussion with your partner where you each take the point of view about which you have read, and argue your case from that point of view. Make sure you both get a chance to state your case – one person talks and the other listens then change. Keep going until you both have finished your side of the argument.

e) Did anyone clearly win the argument?

f) Now swap roles and swap notes.

g) Read the other person's notes and consider their point of view.

h) Discuss the issue again but this time make your argument from the opposing point of view.

i) Does the same side of the argument win?

j) Think about whether you were able to understand the argument from both sides.

k) Did you notice that you felt differently when arguing the two sides, especially the side that you don't believe is right?

EXERCISE 3 – Other people's beliefs

Empathy means being able to understand and appreciate another person's point of view or beliefs. You don't have to agree with their point of view or their beliefs but in order to have empathy with them you have to be able to see the world through their eyes.

a) Consider all the things that you believe – scientific beliefs, family beliefs, cultural beliefs, religious beliefs, etc. Try making a list of some of the things you believe.

b) Now next to each one write down one thing that someone might believe which would be opposite to your belief.

c) For each one try to put yourself into the thinking of someone who believes the thing that is opposite to your belief. What would be important for them? How would they be thinking? How would they feel meeting someone with your beliefs?

d) How difficult is that for you?

Things I believe.

....

....

....

....

Things someone else might believe.

....

....

....

....

EXERCISE 4 – Listening for feelings

In order to empathise we need to learn to listen for clues that tell us how a person is feeling and then recognize and acknowledge those feelings.

a) Work in pairs or as a group.

b) Find a video clip of interesting spoken work poetry or a famous political speech and watch it all through once.

c) Then watch it again, slowly, pausing at the end of each sentence or each section and write down the emotions that you think the person is showing and also the emotional reaction you think was generated in the audience at the time.

Describe the clip:	
Emotions the speaker was showing	**Emotions generated in the audience**
Part 1	
Part 2	
Part 3	
Part 4	
Part 5	

d) Look at what other people have written down.

e) Do you all agree on the emotions being expressed?

Delegation

2c – Delegate and share responsibility for decision making.

<table>
<tr><td>

Mastery

You will know you are at the **Expert** level in the use of this ATL skill when, given a position of responsibility or leadership, you automatically divide tasks up, allocate responsibility for decision making to others and are confident of achieving the desired results.

</td><td>

Delegation means breaking large tasks down into smaller tasks and allocating those smaller tasks to other people, but also providing them with all that they need to be able to make decisions themselves and contribute competently to the completion of the larger task. Effective delegation builds healthy teams by empowering others to contribute and shows that the leader values, and has confidence in, the capabilities of team members to get the job done.

</td></tr>
</table>

Exercise 1 – Organization

Either use a real task that needs organizing at school or imagine that the principal has asked your class to organize a full day of sporting activities for younger students at school, to take place on a Friday in two weeks time.

a. What are all the tasks that have to be completed to make sure such an event is successful?

Get into pairs and breakdown all the tasks needed to organize and successfully complete such an event, including tasks before, during and after the event. Make sure you remember things like equipment, safety, supervision, clean-up, etc.

	BRAINSTORMED IDEAS...	LOGICAL SEQUENCE...
In pairs – brainstorm all the tasks first and then put them into a logical sequence.		

b. Once you think you have finished your task list, join another pair to make a group of four and compare with what another team has written and make one bigger, more complete list out of your two lists.

c. Once you think you have finished your task list, join another four to make a group of eight and compare with what another team has written and make one bigger list out of the two.

---

d. Put all the tasks up on the board or the wall, give each main task a name.
e. Nominate one person as the best person to be the overall supervisor for the day. That person will now take charge of the process.
f. Write the five main tasks into the table below and then as a whole group, guided by the supervisor, you need to make decisions for each task and write them in the table:

Name each key task:	1.	2.	3.	4.	5.
When is the deadline for each task – when would each task need to be finished?					
How long do you think each task would take to complete?					
When would each task need to be started?					
What will be the most critical task – the one without which nothing else can happen?					
How many people do you have available, and how many would need to be allocated to each task?					
Ask people to consider their strengths and put their name next to each task they think they could do.					
The leader now needs to allocate responsibility for the completion of each task to individual class members by name.					

g. The class needs to discuss how they felt about being given responsibility for the completion of tasks.
h. The leader needs to describe how it felt to delegate responsibility to individuals.

Exercise 2 – Creating a team

a) For the next group work task you are set by your teacher, you could try to use delegation to allocate roles and tasks and to form the most effective team.

   First you need to be very clear about that you have been set to complete in a group.

   • What needs to be done – what is the question that needs to be answered?

   • When does the task or project need to be completed?

   • How will successful completion be judged – what is the teacher looking for, how will it be marked, graded, what are the most important criteria of assessment?

b) Define the roles to be taken in the group to complete the task – as many roles as there are team members – and describe what each role involves.

c) Use the roles in the following table or make up your own roles:

ROLES	DESCRIPTION OF ROLES
Team leader	Keeps everyone on task.
Question planner	Breaks the teacher's question down into a sequence of smaller questions and gives those to the Researcher to find information.
Researcher	Finds the correct information to answer the questions.
Recorder	Writes down a summary of all the important points that the researcher finds.
Writer	Takes the key points from the Recorder and organizes them into a draft document. Identifies gaps in understanding and relays the need for new information to the Question Planner.

d) Team members – identify strengths of each team member – what are they good at?

e) Make up a table like below and have each team member write in their name and, in the "Own Strengths" column, what they feel are their strengths that might be useful for this project, (e.g. organizing other people, generating ideas, writing clearly, researching, etc.).

f) Pass the table around and have everyone in the team write in what they see as other team members' strengths in the "As seen by others" column.

Team Member	Own strengths	As seen by others
1.		
2.		
3.		
4.		
5.		
6.		

g) As a whole group, decide first whether roles in the team are going to stay the same for the whole length of the project or if you are going to rotate roles. If you decide to rotate roles, how often you will change?

h) Decide as a whole group who is going to be the team leader.

The team leader's first task is then to decide who will take each role:

i) The team leader allocates roles to individual team members.

j) The team leader makes sure every person has all the resources they need to complete their task.

k) The team leader decides on schedules of work – what do you need to get done by when?

l) The team starts working on the first task.

m) The leader keeps everyone on task.

Once the whole group's work tasks are completed, all members need to give some feedback as to how successful they thought the process was:

n) Discuss how effective the team leader was in allocating tasks, in keeping everyone on task and in supporting team members.

o) What did you learn about effective delegation?

....

....

....

....

....

Helping Others Succeed

2d – Help others to succeed.

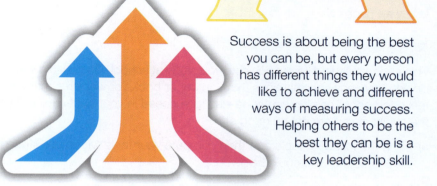

Mastery

You will know you are at the **Expert** level in the use of this ATL skill when you can confidently gauge what others see as success and assist them to achieve their success.

Success is about being the best you can be, but every person has different things they would like to achieve and different ways of measuring success. Helping others to be the best they can be is a key leadership skill.

Exercise 1 – What is success?

a. Work with a partner and make a list of all the ways someone could be successful in this world.

....

....

....

b. Imagine it is 20 years from now and you have achieved what you think of as success. What would give you that feeling? How would you measure your own success in 20 years' time?

....

....

....

c. Then think about what would be success for you in 10 years time, in 5 years time and by the end of this year. What would indicate to you that you were successful at these times? At each point also consider what you need to do before then to achieve that success and how anyone else could possibly help you and fill in the following table:

Success	By the end of this year	In 5 years' time	In 10 years' time
How would you know if you had achieved success for you?			
What would you need to have done before then to achieve the success you desire?			
How could someone else help you to achieve what you want to achieve?			

d. Swap pages with your partner.

e. Write all the things you could do for your partner this year that would help him or her to move closer to his or her goal for success for the end of this year.

....

....

....

f. Swap pages back.

Exercise 2 – Helping others learn successfully

Think about all the different subjects you study at school. Do you find some to be easier to learn than others? In your best subjects do you have any special things that you do, or books or websites that you use, which seem to make it easier for you? Would you feel good about helping someone else to succeed in your best subject? Would it be useful for you if someone else helped you in the subjects you are not so good at?

a) Fill in the following table and then compare your table with other students in your class until you find someone you could help and someone who could help you.

My best subject is:	I think I do well in this subject because…	The best resources I have found that help me with this subject are…	I could help someone else in this subject by…
The subject I have the most difficulty with is:	I think I have difficulty in this subject because…	The resources that I have for this subject are…	I could do with some help in this subject with…

Exercise 3 – Study teams

The single thing that research has shown will improve student learning more than any other factor, is students teaching other students. Study teams work!

a) Once you have finished Exercise 2 see if you can organize a team of 3 or 4 students who are interested in working together and helping each other to succeed.

b) See if you can put together a study team where each person has a strength in a different subject.

c) All members of your study team need to have a similar goal – to succeed at school to the best of their ability.

d) Arrange to meet on a regular basis – how often can you get together, where and when?

e) Make sure you have each other's contact details – a way to get in touch if you have a problem or a question you can't answer.

f) When you meet as a study team you each need to come up with one question or something you don't understand in a subject and ask for help. All the other team members then need to try to explain that thing to you in words you will understand, or help you find and use good resources to make sense of what you don't yet understand.

g) Work together, help each other.

h) Remember TEAM means: **T**ogether
    Everyone
    Achieves
    More

Taking Responsibility

2e – Take responsibility for your actions.

Mastery

You will know you are at the **Expert** level in the use of this ATL skill when you consistently and automatically assume full responsibility for everything that you think, say and do.

Taking full responsibility for your actions involves being honest with yourself and making yourself accountable. Being accountable means accepting all the consequences of your own actions and being prepared to change if your actions don't turn out well.

Taking responsibility also means ensuring that your actions are fair for those people with whom you are in contact, and are ethically sound (e.g. cause no environmental harm).

Exercise 1 – Responsibility, acceptability and consequences

a) Work individually at first.

b) Consider what your responsibilities are at home, at school and in your community; what actions you could take; and what might be the consequences of not taking such actions.

d) Work in pairs and compare responses for each situation with someone else.

e) Did you come up with the same actions and consequences?

f) If not, discuss the differences.

	For each situation, what are responsibilities you have	What are responsible and acceptable actions?	What are the consequences of not taking responsibility?
At home	• e.g. feeding the cat • • • • • •	• doing it daily at right time • • • • • •	• cat runs away to find food elsewhere • • • • • •
At school	• e.g. listening actively in class • • • • • •	• concentrating in every class • • • • • •	• learning progress suffers • • • • • •
In the community	• e.g. contributing to events • • • • • •	• volunteering to help • • • • • •	• less social connection • • • • • •

Exercise 2 – Actions and consequences

g) Work individually at first.

h) Consider what are safe and responsible actions you could take in each of the following situations, and what might be the consequences of not taking such actions?

i) Having done all of the following, write in a few of your own situations which are relevant to your life and complete the table

j) Work in pairs and compare responses for each situation with someone else.

k) Did you come up with the same actions and consequences?

l) If not, discuss the differences.

Situation	What are the responsible and safe actions you could take in each situation?	What might be the consequences of not taking responsibility?
Crossing road while on your phone		
Climbing a ladder		
Doing jobs around the house		
Being offered drugs, cigarettes or alcohol		
Being confronted by an angry person		
Being involved in risk-taking activities with peer group		
Swimming in the sea, lakes, rivers or pools		
Being approached by a stranger		
Helping someone who is bleeding		
Handling poisonous materials		
Being out in the sun		

Resolving Conflict

2f – Manage and Resolve conflict and work collaboratively in teams.

Mastery

You will know you are at the **Expert** level in the use of this ATL skill when you are able to resolve any conflict effectively to the satisfaction of all parties involved.

A conflict is more than just a disagreement. It is a situation in which one or both parties perceive a threat (whether or not the threat is real). We respond to conflicts based on our perceptions of the situation, not necessarily to an objective review of the facts. Our perceptions are influenced by our life experiences, culture, values, and beliefs. Conflicts trigger strong emotions. Conflicts are an opportunity for growth. When you're able to resolve conflict in a relationship, it builds trust.

Exercise 1 – Manage and resolve conflict

The most important thing to do to help resolve any conflict is to take the emotional heat out of the conflict and deal with the issue rationally. This is sometimes difficult to do but an analytical approach can often help.

To do the next exercise you could either set up a conflict situation as a role play or wait for a real conflict to develop.

In either case you need to identify an issue about which two people or two groups feel strongly (with which they have an emotional engagement) and on which they have opposing viewpoints, but one they are both interested in resolving.

Then work both parties through the following analysis, asking them to clearly explain or write down the answers at each step:

	Person (or group) A viewpoint	Person (or group) B viewpoint
Describe the issue – what are the facts?		
Describe your emotional engagement with the issue – about what aspects of this issue do you feel most strongly?		
Why do you think you have a conflict over this issue?		
On what aspects of the conflict do you both agree?		

What would be a solution to this problem that would totally meet your needs?		
What would be the worst thing that could happen?		
For what aspects of this conflict are you prepared to take responsibility?		
Each party describe something the other party could do to overcome some of the emotional heat of the conflict.	What they could do is …..	What they could do is ….
Are you prepared to take the action described by the other party?		
Over what aspects of the conflict are you prepared to negotiate?		
If anything were possible, what might an imaginative solution be?		
What is a way forward, an action on which you both agree that would help you both to move closer to overcoming this conflict?		
Was this process useful to you as a means of dealing with conflict?		

Exercise 2 – Work collaboratively in teams

Groups and teams often form spontaneously in social, sporting, school or cultural settings, or are set up deliberately by facilitators or teachers to achieve specific purposes.

In all cases, achieving effective collaboration is a complex mix of the use of many skills including listening, encouraging, considering other people's viewpoints, contributing your own ideas, negotiating and reaching consensus. These are all ATL skills which can be worked through in the exercises found in *2g – Build consensus; 2i – Listen actively to others perspectives and ideas;* and *2k – Encourage others to contribute* on page 57; *1.1a – Give and receive meaningful feedback,* page 2; *1.1b – Use intercultural understanding to interpret communications,* page 4; *1.1f – Interpret and effectively use modes of non-verbal communication,* page 12; *1.1g – Negotiate ideas and knowledge with peers and teachers,* page 14; *2b – Practice empathy,* page 44. Put all together, these skills will build an excellent framework for collaborative work in teams.

Building Consensus

2g – Build consensus.
2i – Listen actively to others' perspectives and ideas.
2k – Encourage others to contribute.

Mastery

You will know you are at the **Expert** level in the use of this ATL skill set when you are able to collaborate well in teams and groups, listen effectively, build consensus and achieve your individual and group goals.

Active listening means concentrating well and keeping your mind on the topic without drifting off. First you need to work through page 86, *4.1a – Practice focus and concentration.* See *Monitoring your internal conversation* on page 89 to get an understanding of what this means and how to monitor it and *Exercise 8 – Practice mindfulness training* to get better at it.

Exercise 1 – Keep a listening log

a) When you are next in a group work setting you can practice these skills by keeping a log.

b) First, divide up a piece of paper into big squares with one square for each person in the group and where they are sitting (e.g. for 4 people sitting in a square):

PERSON 1

PERSON 2

PERSON 3

PERSON 4

c) Put their names in the correct square.

d) As each person speaks, put one dot next to their name and write in their square:

   i.   their main points – differentiate between facts and opinions (maybe with different colored pens or with an "F" next to a fact and an "O" next to an opinion), also put a check or a cross next to each main point depending on whether you agree with it or not

   ii. your impression of how they feel about what they are saying – comfortable, uncomfortable, worried, happy, etc.

   iii. any suggestions they make of things other people could do

   iv. any questions you think of that relate to what they are saying.

e) keeping these things in mind and writing them down while you are listening will increase your concentration and help you develop more active listening.

Exercise 2 – Encouraging others

a) While you are making your listening log you will automatically be tracking how many contributions each group member makes.

b) If one or two people are dominating the discussion or one or two people are not participating, at an appropriate moment – when the talker pauses in their delivery – interrupt with something like:

   i.   "That's really interesting, what do other people think about that point?"

   ii. "What do you think about that ... (a person's name)?"

   iii. "We need to make sure that everyone in the group is heard so what do the rest of you think?"

c) When you have succeeded in getting a reluctant speaker to voice their opinion make sure you listen really well and praise them for participating and then paraphrase back what they have said, ask them a question or ask them to explain further. Try and draw them more into the discussion: "You make a good point ..."

   i.   "Tell me more about that?"

   ii. "Did I get it right – are you saying that ... ?"

   iii. "Can you tell me more about your experience with this?"

   iv. "Can you explain more about ... ?"

Exercise 3 – Building consensus

A consensus is a decision reached by a group as a whole. Not everyone has to agree with every part of the decision but to have consensus everyone needs to agree on a course of action to move forward.

a) Make sure everyone is involved in the discussion and everyone has had a chance to say what they think – if you use a listening log this is easy to ensure.

b) Make sure everyone's idea has equal weight – not the loudest being the most important.

c) Work towards a solution through collaboration and cooperation between all group members.

d) Look at the strengths and weaknesses of all possible solutions.

e) Try to build an overall solution or action plan which has input from every group member.

f) If no consensus can be reached, separate areas of agreement from areas of disagreement and see if you can get a consensus decision about the areas that are agreed on.

g) Make sure that once a consensus decision is reached, all group members get to comment on it.

Fairness and Equity

2h – Make fair and equitable decisions.

Mastery

You will know you are at the **Expert** level in the use of this ATL skill when you can automatically look at any situation or issue and judge what are the points to be considered that underpin fair decisions for everyone involved.

Any decisions made can advantage some people and disadvantage others. The aim is for all decisions to be fair so that everyone is on an equal footing with equal outcomes.

Look carefully at any situation or issue to first identify all the people who will be affected by the decision that needs to be made. Then consider what things will advantage or disadvantage them. Obviously there will be some not so good things that are unavoidable, but most people will accept these if they believe the process has been fair for all concerned.

Exercise 1 – Decision making at school

a) Imagine that your teacher has permission to take your class on a field trip for your favorite subject in two months' time and has two options for a possible destination – one within your country and one in another country. You and a partner have been asked to consider all the important factors and make the decision on where to go.

b) Discuss this situation with a partner and work through the following table to reach a fair and equitable decision.

What factors need to be considered? For example, cost, student enjoyment, learning objectives, etc.	How important is each one to the students? Mark each one high, medium or low importance.	How important is each one for the teacher? Mark each one high, medium or low importance.	Considering the information gathered, put all the factors into an overall priority from most important to least important.

What is the decision that you think is fair and equitable for everyone?

Justify your answer – on what basis is this decision fair and equitable to everyone?

How difficult is it to make decisions that are fair and equitable for everyone?

Exercise 2 – Decision making at home

Think of a situation or issue at home where a decision needs to be made which affects everyone in the family and where there are two clear options (e.g. two choices of places to go on vacation). Complete the following table to enable you to make a fair and equitable decision.

Describe the issue or situation and identify the two options:			
What factors need to be considered? For example, cost, enjoyment, use of time, effect on schoolwork, etc.	How important is each one to the children in the family? Mark each one high, medium or low importance.	How important is each one for the parents or caregivers in the family? Mark each one high, medium or low importance.	Considering the information gathered, put all the factors into an overall priority from most important to least important.

What is the decision that you think is fair and equitable for everyone?

Justify your answer – on what basis is this decision fair and equitable to everyone?

How difficult is it to make decisions that are fair and equitable for everyone?

Leadership

2l – Exercise leadership and take on a variety of roles within groups.

Mastery

You will know you are at the **Expert** level in the use of this ATL skill when others naturally turn to you to lead in most situations.

Leadership is a natural thing for some people and a learned skill for others. Anyone can learn how to lead and it is a very valuable skill to practice – particularly in a group learning situation.

Work through *2i – Listen actively to others' perspectives and ideas, 2k – Encourage others to contribute* and *2g – Build consensus* on page 57 first, to get a good idea of how to be an active member of any group and take on whatever roles are appropriate.

Also all of the following ATL skill exercises will teach you some of the effective skills important in good leaders. Work your way through all of them first:

> *4.2 Perseverance* on page 90;
> *4.4 Self-Motivation* on page 101;
> *4.5 Resilience* on page 107.

Exercise 1 – Leadership attitude

Leadership by example means willingly and positively taking on the hardest tasks – the most difficult jobs, the things that have the greatest responsibility, that no-one else wants to do – in order to demonstrate to other people that anything is possible. This requires a leader to overcome his or her own fears and uncertainties, develop a "can do" attitude and demonstrate that attitude in everyday life. The best way to do that is simply to practice at every opportunity.

What are some of the opportunities in your life to demonstrate leadership? In each situation below think about what you could do, voluntarily, ...

	What would be your greatest fear in doing this?	How will you overcome that fear?
At school, in subject classes, I could ...		
At school, outside the classroom, I could ...		
At home, I could ...		
One other place or situation where I could practice my leadership skills is...		

Exercise 2 – Who would you follow?

In some ways the characteristics of a great leader are the same as characteristics of the perfect big sister or the perfect big brother, e.g. kindness, common sense, etc. The sort of person that you could trust, that you would follow anywhere. Leaders are people that other people naturally want to follow.

a) Work with a partner and brainstorm what these characteristics might be and then fill in the other two columns:

List the characteristics of the "perfect" big brother or big sister.	What is one example of something they might do which would demonstrate this characteristic?	Think of one opportunity you each could take to demonstrate that same characteristic.
e.g. Kindness	Help someone younger with their homework.	Go and see the .... teacher and volunteer to give up one lunchtime this week to help a younger student who is struggling.

Exercise 3 – Vision and action

Leaders are also people who are visionary – they can imagine the world the way they think it could be – and they are also people who take action to try to solve problems and bring about the perfect world the way they can see it.

a) Identify a problem in your local environment – at your school, at home, in your city or your local community – something that is making life more difficult for someone or some group of people.

b) Gather information and evidence about the real nature of the problem.

c) Come up with a plan to help alleviate the problem.

d) Break the plan down into steps.

e) Gather support for your plan from others.

f) Work out what you need to do to take the first step in your plan.

g) Get it done.

The problem as I see it is	
The people who are most affected by this are	
The evidence I have collected is	
I think the solution to the problem is	
To get my solution working, the steps that need to be taken are	1.
	2.
	3.
	4.
	5.
To get the first step happening I will need to	To whom will you need to talk and enlist their help?
	What resources will you need?
	When will the first step need to be completed?
Once the first step is done what needs to happen next?	

Advocating Rights

2n – Advocate for one's own rights and needs.

Mastery

You will know you are at the **Expert** level in the use of this ATL skill when you can confidently represent yourself and speak up for your rights and needs.

In all areas of your life, you have different rights and associated responsibilities. A "right" is defined as a "moral or legal entitlement." For example, in most countries all children have a right to education – a right to go to school and to become educated. A right is not something that only applies to some people, a right is something that applies to everyone. Understanding what your moral and legal rights are in all situations enables you to monitor what you are doing and to speak up for your rights.

You also have needs to be met which vary from situation to situation. It is important to distinguish between what are your needs and what are your wants. Sometimes people speak up for what they want, not so much for what they need.

Exercise 1 – Children's rights

a) Work with a partner and research the UN Convention on the Rights of the Child (you can find an easy-to-understand version through UNICEF).

b) Discuss these rights with your partner, pick out what you see as the ten most important rights and write them in the table below.

c) Write in the countries that have ratified these rights and those that haven't yet.

Ten top Rights of the Child	Countries that have ratified all these rights	Countries that haven't yet ratified all these rights
1.		
2.		
3.		
4.		
5.		
6.		
7.		
8.		
9.		
10.		

d) If your country is one of the ones that hasn't yet ratified these rights, what could you do about that?

Exercise 2 – Rights and needs at school

Work with a partner and discuss each of the following points. See if you can reach agreement on each of them and write your answers in the following table. Write down what your rights and needs are at school. Then consider how important each of them is and what you could say, and to whom, to advocate for each of them.

a) First you need to determine what your rights at school are – these may well be a mixture of moral and legal rights and can probably be found in one of the official documents at school. Check with your website and your school charter or mission statement and any other official school foundation documents to see if you can find what your rights at your school are.

What are your rights at school? For example, your right to learn, to be safe, etc.	How important is this right to you? Rate it as low, medium or high.	How important do you think this right is to your school? Rate it as low, medium or high.	If you weren't being given this right, to whom would you need to present a case to try to gain this right? Who has the power to grant this right?	What would be your argument for being granted this right? What evidence would you need to gather and what would you need to say?

b) In this part it is important to distinguish between your wants and your needs. You might want lunchtime to last for three hours each day but that is not a need. You have a need to become educated and informed.

What are your needs at school? For example, your need for a chair, warm classrooms.	How important is this need to you? Rate it as low, medium or high.	How important is this need to your school? Rate it as low, medium or high.	If this need was not being met, to whom would you need to present a case to try to get this need met? Who has the power to grant this?	What would be your argument for getting this need met? What evidence would you need to gather and what would you need to say?

Exercise 3 – Rights and needs with friends

Work with a partner and discuss each of the following points, see if you can reach agreement on each of them and write your answers in the following table. Write down what your rights and needs are in your social group, with your friends. Then consider how important each of them is and what you could say to advocate for each of them.

a) One place to find what your rights as an individual are is in documents like the Universal Declaration of Human Rights or the Universal Declaration of the Rights of the Child which can be found on the United Nations website.

What are your rights in your friendship group? For example, your right to listened to, to be safe.	How important is this right to you? Rate it as low, medium or high.	How important is this right to your friendship group? Rate it as low, medium or high.	If you weren't being given this right, how could you create a conversation to receive it? What would you say to speak up for this right?

b) In this part it is important to distinguish between your wants and your needs. You might want all your friends to always do everything you say but that is not a need. You have a need to be listened to and respected.

What are your needs in your friendship group? For example, your need for company, for sharing highs and lows.	How important is this need to you? Rate it as low, medium or high.	How important is this need to your friendship group? Rate it as low, medium or high.	If this need was not being met how could you create a case to receive it? What would you say to speak up for this need?

Self-Assessment of ATL Skills

To see how best to use this page refer to pages 114 and 115.

ATL Skills	Novice *Watch*	Learner *Copy*	Practitioner *Do*				Expert *Share*
			Starting	*Practicing*	*Getting better*	*Got it!*	
Empathy							
Delegation							
Helping Others Succeed							
Taking Responsibility							
Resolving Conflict							
Building Consensus							
Fairness and Equity							
Leadership							
Advocating Rights							

Student Self-Assessment of ATL Skills Proficiency – COLLABORATION SKILLS

Notes

ORGANIZATION SKILLS

To organize means to arrange in a systematic and orderly manner. The process of organizing involves planning, structuring, integrating and co-ordinating tasks, goals and activities to unite effort in order to attain objectives.

Organizing is a logical process that usually starts with a goal and a deadline, which inevitably leads to an awareness of the resources needed to achieve that goal, then to aligning those resources with a timeline necessary to achieve the goal by or before the deadline.

At school you will find that much of the organization is done for you – who teaches you, when, where and what they teach you, how they teach you, when and how they set deadlines for assignments, tests and exams are pre-arranged and you do not need to be involved in organizing any of it. Unfortunately, this lack of involvement in organizing your own life at school sometimes leads some students into thinking there is no point in organizing any of their own tasks because "teachers will always remind me." But if you look at the best students in any school you will always find they are very well organized. They know how to prioritize tasks, they know how to find the resources they need to complete projects and assignments and they know how to get things done on time or even before the deadline, and somehow they always seem to have plenty of time to do the things they like to do as well. You might also find that less successful students are often stressed, pressured, late with everything, feel overwhelmed most of the time and never seem to have any time to do the things they really want to do. The difference is simply organization.

Through practicing the skills in this cluster you will get better at organizing all the information you get at school, better at using technology to help you find the information you want, and better at planning out all your work so you meet all your deadlines easily.

In this cluster you will also find the skills you need to achieve all your own goals. Not just how to set goals – that is easy – but also the secrets of how to get yourself to overcome procrastination, to take action and to take all the steps you need to take to achieve all your goals.

GREAT ORGANIZATION

Every four years there are two Olympic Games held somewhere in the world – the Summer and the Winter Olympics – involving over 13,000 athletes competing in 33 different sports and nearly 400 events. The organization of such huge events involves many thousands of people and many millions of individual tasks and starts seven years before – three years before the previous games!

The Organizing Committee of each Olympic Games is responsible for organizing not only the facilities for each sport and the accommodations and transport for all athletes, coaches, officials, media people and the public who come to see the games, but, especially in modern times, the committee is also responsible for the safety and security of everyone involved in any aspect of the games.

The organization of any Olympic Games is an enormous task but the skills required to do it are the same skills that anyone needs to organize any event – goal setting, planning, resourcing, time-lining and "getting stuff done!"

Deadlines

3a – Plan short-term and long-term assignments; meet deadlines.
3c – Keep and use a weekly planner for assignments.
3d – Set goals that are challenging and realistic.

Mastery

You will know you are at the **Expert** level in the use of this ATL skill set when, as soon as a teacher gives you a new assignment deadline (or you create your own goal), you automatically break that deadline down into stages, you mark all those stages on your calendar and you get each stage done on time – without anyone else reminding you.

Exercise 1 – Assignment timetabling

The biggest problem most students have with getting assignments done is procrastination – putting things off until the last minute. When you do this of course you feel the pressure, you suffer from stress, you start to panic and then you put in an 'all-nighter' to get it done. Unfortunately by doing things this way you don't do your best work, you don't get the marks you want and you feel bad about that, which doesn't help your stress levels and so it goes on. You always do your best work when you take your time, you research all aspects thoroughly, you plan your writing properly and you write well. The secret to overcoming procrastination is organization, and of course everyone tells you to be organized but maybe no-one has shown you a few simple strategies that will help. This is one of the most important ATL skills to help you survive school and succeed well.

There are three parts to this skill – the first is planning all your schoolwork out well in advance, the second is setting realistic goals and the third is getting yourself to take action on your goals and stick to your schedule (for the last see page 74 **3e – Plan strategies and take action to achieve personal and academic goals**).

a) Buy or make a full-year paper calendar – one that covers all the months of your full school year, big enough to go on the wall in front of your desk where you do your schoolwork at home and big enough so that you can write all your plans and goals on it. First put on it:

   i. whole school year with all term dates and holidays, any major sports events, social events, any known test and exam dates.

   ii. when a teacher gives you an assignment, put the date in your phone then as soon as you get home transfer that completion date to your year planner.

   iii. timeline every assignment – break each one down into stages.

b) Work out for yourself, what are the key stages of completing any assignment and what proportion of any assignment does each stage take?

   i. Research – finding the information. What proportion of any assignment does the research phase take? 25%? You decide for yourself.

   ii. Processing the information – reading all the information you have gathered, cutting and pasting useful quotes, summarizing key points (see page 33 **1.2i and 1.2j – Effective notes**). 25% of the time?

   iii. Planning the piece of work – sequencing ideas into a logical flow that is going to meet the assignment objectives and present your own point of view well. 5%?

   iv. Doing the writing – always the stage that takes the longest, pulling together all your research, key points, quotes, re-writing all your cut and pasted material into your own words and developing your own well substantiated argument – 40%?

   v. Proof reading, making corrections and handing it in – 5%?

c) You have now created five separate deadlines for each assignment instead of just one terminal deadline. Mark each one on your year planner.

d) Make the date for completing each part of any assignment a serious deadline for yourself – "due in tomorrow" – create some urgency within yourself for getting each deadline completed.

e) Make up a weekly schedule at the beginning of each week with all your deadlines for every assignment and all your sports, extra-curricula and social events.

f) Make up a weekly or daily "To Do" list and get things done! Cross them off when they are done (see below).

g) Do a small amount on every pending assignment EVERY DAY!

h) Always remember to build in some sort of celebration for yourself for the successful completion of major pieces of work.

Exercise 2 – Managing the achievement of other goals

No doubt you have other goals as well – apart from academic goals – maybe in music, dance, drama, sports, leisure, general fitness, health, relationships. For any of your goals that are not strictly academic or connected directly with school, the process of setting goals is still the same:

a) First become very clear about exactly what your goal is. Try writing it out using the POSITIVE framework. Is your goal:

   i. **P**ositive language – make sure you write your goal focused on what you want to achieve, not what you want to avoid – not to "stop procrastinating" but to "manage your time better"

   ii. **O**utcome-focused – describe what the finished goal, the outcome, will look like or be like

   iii. **S**pecific – get very specific about exactly what you want to achieve, make sure the goal is tangible, measurable

   iv. **I**nspirational – make sure your goal is a step you are taking towards something that inspires you, something that you really want

   v. **T**imed – create a realistic timeline for the completion of this goal, how long will it take to get to the end?

   vi. **I**ncentive – make sure you have built in something to look forward to when you have achieved this goal, a reward, an incentive

   vii. **V**isualize – use your imagination to visualize yourself achieving this goal, picture your successful completion of this goal in your mind

   viii. **E**valuate – build in stages of evaluation of progress towards your goal, how will you know when you are ¼ completed, half-way there, etc.?

b) Break each goal down into achievable steps.

c) Work out when you want to get every step done by.

d) Mark each step on your calendar.

e) Get the first step done today!

Exercise 3 – Making "To-Do" lists

"To-Do" lists are simply lists of all the things you need to get done in a certain time frame. You can make a new one once a day or every couple of days or once a week – up to you – but they need to be re-visited and updated on a daily basis. Make one now.

a) Get a clean sheet of paper, write TO DO at the top and write a list of all the tasks you have at the moment – all the things you need to get done in the next week or so. List every task, not in general terms like "homework" but as specific tasks like "math assignment," "football practice."

b) Then next to each one write in a date – when will you be doing that thing (volleyball practice) or when you want to have each one done by (Biology assignment)?

c) Then write in next to each one how long you estimate it will take to complete each task – be realistic!

Your tasks on the list will probably be of two types – scheduled tasks like music lessons or sports practice that happen at times set by others, and unscheduled tasks like school assignments for which you only have deadlines by which time they need to be completed.

d) For all your scheduled tasks, go to your weekly planner and make sure they are all written in at the correct time. If they are things that happen away from home or school, make sure you have included enough time to get there and home again.

e) For all your unscheduled tasks make up a priority order. Number them from No. 1 for the most important task – most urgent and most significant for you – No. 2 second, etc.

f) Start with task 1 now! See *4.2a – Demonstrate persistence and perseverance* and *4.2b – Practice delaying gratification* on page 90 for ways to get yourself to persist until each task is complete.

g) As soon as you have finished any task, cross it off your To Do list.

h) Update your To Do list or make a new one on a daily basis.

Exercise 4 – Taking action

Getting yourself to take the actions needed to achieve your goals is a specific skill in itself. Go to page 74 and do the exercises for *3e – Plan strategies and take action to achieve personal and academic goals.*

Exam Timetabling

3b – Create plans to prepare for summative assessments.

Mastery

You will know you are at the **Expert** level in the use of this ATL skill when you have created a good study timetable, put it up on the wall in a prominent place and are actively sticking to your schedule of study.

Creating a Plan for Exams:

Studying effectively and studying enough prior to any summative assessments (exams) are the two things that are in your control that can have the greatest effect on your exam performance and ultimately your exam grade. One of the key strategies to help with this is making an exam study timetable, the other is sticking to your timetable (see this exercise for the first and *3e – Plan strategies and take action to achieve personal and academic goals* on page 74, for the second).

Exercise 1 – Making an exam study timetable

a) About two months before the beginning of your exams create a calendar that covers the two months prior and every day until the end of your final exam.

b) Write in the dates and times for all your exams.

c) Now you have to make four important decisions:

    i.   Are you going to do some study for these exams?

    ii. If so when are you going to start studying?

    iii. Are you going to study every day from your start date to the end of the final exam or are you going to give yourself some days off? My advice would be that you do give yourself some time off each week but not more than one day off per week. Also, if you have school vacation in the time between now and your last exam, it is ok to take some of your vacation off to have a holiday, but not more than half of your vacation off.

    iv. On each day that you have decided you are going to study, how many hours are you prepared to put into study?

d) On your calendar, cross out the days you aren't going to study and write in on each day that is left how many hours you are prepared to commit to study on that day. I am not talking about studying continuously without breaks, though – you need to take lots of breaks. But, for example, if you had a full day available – maybe a Saturday – you could easily get 2 hours done in the morning, 2 hours in the afternoon and 2 hours in the evening – 6 hours study and you have still had most of the day off.

The trick is to make time for study your highest priority each day from now until the end of your last exam and get it done first before you do the other things you really want to do. Remember that effort is one of the few factors you have in your control and effort can be measured in hours.

e) Add up your total study hours.

f) Prioritize all your exam subjects with the subject that you know you need to put the most time and effort into at the top of the list, the one you know needs the least amount of time from you at the bottom and all the other subjects arranged in-between.

g) Divide up the total study time available between all your subjects, making sure you give more time to the subjects at the top of the list and less time to each subject down the list. Make sure that the total study time is the same as the total time calculated in Step e.

h) Write in which subjects to study each night in 1-2 hour chunks. So, if you only have 1 hour available on any day just study 1 subject; 2 hours maybe 2 subjects – one hour each; 4 hours maybe two subjects, 2 hours per subject. Make sure you are studying each subject at least once each week and that your numbers add up correctly.

How to check that you have enough time available to get through all the work you need to do?

i) Get a copy of the syllabus (or curriculum) for each subject you are going to be studying and add up the total number of topics you are going to need to review before the exams.

j) Divide the total number of topics to study in each subject by the hours available for study in that subject – this will give you a rough guide of the study rate you need in topics/hour.

k) When you start studying in accordance with your study timetable, take a note of how many topics you get through in the hours that you study.

l) Work out if you have enough time in your timetable to get through all the topics you need to get through before the exam.

m) If there is not enough time in your timetable either process the information faster or add in more time. If there is more time than you need – take time out.

Make your timetable a "living" document.

n) If, on any particular day, you find that you don't get the hours of study done that you planned, for whatever reason, the most important thing to do is transfer the hours you didn't get done to another day. Make sure that you stick to your goals for study time in each subject.

Your study timetable needs to always be a flexible, changeable schedule that helps you to achieve your goals and fits in with your life.

STUDY TIMETABLE

Monday	Tuesday	Wednesday	Thursday	Friday	Saturday	Sunday
				18	19	20
					3 Ela/Bio/DT	3 Ma/BS
14 1 BS	15 1 Bio	16 1 Ph	17 1 Ela	25	26 4 Ch/His	27 4 Ma/Ela
21 1 Ela	22 2 Ch	23 1 Bio	24 2 Eng	1 APRIL	2 5 Ch/His/BS	3 5 Eng/Ph
28 2 Ma	29 2 DT	30 2 Eng	31 2 Ph	8	9 Holidays start	10
4 2 His	5 2 Ma	6 2 Eng	7 2 Ch	15	16	17
11 5 Eng/Ela/Ph	12 5 Eng/Bio/DT	13 5 Ch/His/BS	14 5 Ma/El/DT	22	23	24 Holidays end
18 5 Ch/Bio/BS	19 5 Ela/Ph/DT	20 5 Eng/Ma/BS	21 5 Ch/His/Ph	29	30 5 Eng/Ma/Bio	1 MAY 5 Ch/Ela/BS
25 2 Bio	26 2 Ma	27 2 Ch	28 2 Eng	6	7	8
2 6 Eng/His/Ph	3 MYP Exams	4	5			

Achieving Goals

3e – Plan strategies and take action to achieve personal and academic goals.

Mastery

You will know you are at the **Expert** level in the use of this ATL skill when you always take all the steps necessary to achieve your goals.

Achieving Your Goals:

Setting goals in any aspect of your life is easy – anyone can do that. It is getting yourself to take all the steps necessary to achieve those goals that is a bit more complicated. This is the key strategy for performance improvement – academically, socially, in sports, music, personal growth – wherever and whatever you want to improve. Creating goals and writing them out clearly is important, but it is taking the action necessary to achieve every step that is absolutely critical. And how do you get yourself to do that? First you need to recognize that performance improvement is all about doing things differently than how you have done them up to now – if you were already doing it, you wouldn't need to set a goal to achieve it, would you? To achieve any goal you need to:

1) recognize some dissatisfaction

2) develop a new purpose

3) align your values and beliefs to generate the motivation necessary to bring about change

4) work out what has stopped you taking action to achieve this goal in the past

5) create a new action plan.

Exercise 1 – Achieving your goals

a) Draw up a big table like the example below – 5 rows and 12 columns – with these headings and enough room to write a few things in each box.

Area	Goal	Purpose	Values	Beliefs	Pain	Pleasure	Cost	Benefits	Feelings	Musts	Habits

b) In the **Area** column write in five areas of your life in which you think you would like to achieve new goals – academics at school, sports, relationships, performance arts, physically, emotionally.

c) In the **Goal** column, for each area, write in one goal that you would like to achieve by the end of this year.

d) **Purpose** column – why do you want to achieve that particular goal – what will it lead to, and why do you want to achieve that – what will that lead to. Keep asking that question until you reach your highest purpose for each goal. Write that in.

e) In order to achieve your goals, you need to think about what you value and what you believe and make sure that both of these things help you to achieve your present goals.

   i. Values – this means what things do you see as important in your life that will help you to achieve your goals. Do you value persistence, perseverance, determination, hard work; or do you value relaxing, chilling out, putting things off until tomorrow. Both are sometimes useful but which do you need to value more highly to help you achieve your goals? In the **Values** column write in several important values for each of your goals. Are they the same? Do they all fit well with each other?

ii. Beliefs – this means what you need to believe in order to achieve your goals? Obviously, the first thing you need to believe is that it is possible for you to achieve each of your goals. What else? Do you also need to believe you can find the time, the energy, the motivation to achieve each goal? What else? In the **Beliefs** column write in what it will be necessary for you to believe in order to achieve each of your goals.

f) Motivational forces – motivation can be described as energy directed towards achieving a goal. So how do you generate the necessary energy to achieve all your goals and why haven't you done this already? Why are these goals new for you and not something you have already achieved? All human beings are motivated primarily by two drives – to achieve pleasure and to avoid pain. What you need to consider now is the pleasure you have enjoyed and the pain you have avoided in the past from not pushing yourself to achieve these goals, and then work on flipping that around and consider the pain you will avoid and the pleasure you will generate in the future by making a commitment to achieving all of your new goals.

What you need to do now is in the next five columns write in for each of your goals:

   i. What is the **Pain** you are associating right now with making this change and achieving this goal? Hard work, effort, lack of social life, physical pain, emotional pain, having to get organized, manage your time better, study, etc.?

ii. What is the **Pleasure** you will gain by not following through on achieving this goal? Chilling out, relaxing, not stressing, not feeling any pressure, having more time for yourself, more movies, more social life, etc.?

iii. What will it **Cost** you not to follow through on achieving your goals now? Disappointment, lack of drive and motivation, being unfit, lazy, poor grades, performance, lack of appreciation, poorer future prospects, etc.?

iv. What are the **Benefits** you will gain by following through on achieving all your goals? New potential, more opportunities, better future, more connection, ability to achieve higher goals, enhanced ability to help others, to benefit your community, your friends and family, etc.?

V. What **Feelings** will you have when you achieve each goal? Satisfied, resilient, determined, courageous, worthy, adventurous, motivated, fit, smart, talented, relaxed, relieved, etc.?

"YOU CAN ACHIEVE what the MIND BELIEVES"

g) Action – change only comes through action. So, now you need to consider what actions you need to take to achieve your goals. For each goal there will be things that you could do, things that you should do and things that you must do. Focus on the most critical things – in the **Musts** column write in what the actions are that you will have to take to achieve each goal. List all the things that you must do.

h) Habits and rituals – one of the best ways to get yourself to achieve goals is to create a habit or a ritual that you do every day that moves you one small step closer to achieving your goal. In the **Habits** column write in one thing – even a very small thing – that you will commit to doing every day that moves you one small step closer to achieving your goal, and make a commitment to never miss a day.

i) Leverage – as you know from physics, if you have a lever long enough and a point (fulcrum) on which to balance it you can move a very heavy weight. To achieve your goals you need to get leverage on yourself. There are two ways to do this. Internally – using what you say to yourself and what you visualize – and externally – using the influence of other people.

For all the goals, maybe underneath your table, do the following:

i. Language – create a sentence, a slogan or just a few words, something that you could say to yourself regularly that would help you continue to move towards achieving all your goals.

ii. Visualization – picture yourself at the moment you achieve each of your goals. Close your eyes and imagine yourself in that moment. Notice what you are doing, what you are saying to yourself, to others, how you look, how you feel. Keep refreshing this image by going back to it once a day just for a few minutes and strengthen it – reinforce it in your mind.

iii. Other people – tell as many people as possible about the goals you are going to achieve and ask for their support in helping you achieve all your goals.

Organizing Equipment

3f – Bring necessary equipment and supplies to class.

Mastery

You will know you are at the **Expert** level in the use of this ATL skill when you always arrive at school and to every class, every day with all the right equipment, books, pens and other gear you need to learn well, without anyone preparing it for you.

This is a very simple but important skill which is mostly about predicting what needs to be done and overcoming your tendency to forget things. You are in charge of your learning, no one else. As such, you need to be focused and organized enough to predict what is needed, then make sure you have it before you leave home and before you go to any class.

Exercise 1 – Getting organized

With a partner, brainstorm all the things you need to bring to class for each of your subjects. There will be some items you need for every class.

Items required for all classes	For example your pens, your planner or diary
Subject	**Items for each subject**

Exercise 2 – Creating alarms

a) In your homework diary/planner or on your phone, make up a weekly school lesson schedule or timetable.

b) From your brainstorm in Exercise 1, for each lesson write in what teachers will expect you to bring to class.

c) Set up an alarm system – on your phone, with sticky notes stuck on your bag the night before or written in your diary/planner – to remind yourself every morning what you need to bring for the whole day.

d) Take responsibility for your own actions and don't rely on anyone else to do your thinking for you.

Organizing Files

3g – Keep an organized and logical system of information files/notebooks.
3h – Use appropriate strategies for organizing complex information.

Mastery

You will know you are at the **Expert** level in the use of this ATL skill when you automatically organize all your information and logically record and file it so you can find it later.

At school every day you get a lot of information given to you and you generate a lot of information. You need to have a way to organize and store it so that you can retrieve what you want when you want it. You also get a lot of information through texts, emails and social media messaging. Most of this is already organized though contacts, but some of it you may need to store in a way that enables you to find what you want when you want it.

Exercise 1 – File trees

On your computer you have many different types of information that you want to be able to store and go back to:

- website addresses - links to useful sites for schoolwork, video clips, useful news services, blogs, documentaries

- emails from school, teachers, parents, friends, subscriptions, etc.

If you just let all these build up in your inbox or in your website history it will be easy to lose them and difficult to find what you want when you want it. The best way to overcome that is to create file trees.

a) Set up three file trees – one in your email inbox, one on your web browser and one for all your word processing documents.

b) In all three cases think of all the categories or headings under which the information you want to keep could be stored, and set up one folder for each category.

c) Break each category down into sub-categories with folders within folders.

d) Move all your saved emails, important URLs and all your written documents into the correct folders.

e) Make your categorizing system work the way you think. Whenever you want to store something new, think "if I had forgotten where I put this, where would I look first?" and put it there. If there isn't a place yet, make a new folder in the right place and put it in there.

f) Try to process every piece of information just once – find it, use it, store it.

Exercise 2 – Organizing subject notes

a) Ask each of your subject teachers for a copy of their course outline or find it on the school website or on-line. Print it out, go through it and highlight all the main topic headings and sub-headings.

b) Make up a storage system for each subject that suits the information you gather in that subject – a "ring binder" or series of plastic sleeves for loose pages, labelled exercise books for your own notes.

c) Create one file for each main topic in each subject and a categorization system for all the sub-headings – maybe using sticky notes, colored dividers, colored marker pens.

d) Store the information in the right place as you collect it.

e) Try to process every piece of information just once – find it, use it, store it.

Exercise 3 – Dealing with complex information

Taking all the information from every subject and creating summaries in the way that works best for you is an important step in creating understanding and remembering well.

Work through *1.2i – Note-making* (p.33); *1.2g – Paraphrasing* (p.29); *3i – Learning preferences* (p.79) and *6e – Memory techniques* (p.130) to understand best how to do this.

Learning Preferences

3i – Understand and use sensory learning preferences (learning styles).
5a – Develop new skills, techniques and strategies for effective learning.
5b – Identify strengths and weaknesses of personal learning strategies (self-assessment).
5c – Demonstrate flexibility in the selection and use of learning strategies.
5g – Consider personal learning strategies.
6d – Understand the benefits and limitations of personal sensory learning preferences when accessing, processing and recalling information.

Mastery

You will know you are at the **Expert** level in the use of this ATL skill set when you automatically set yourself up in the classroom and at home to concentrate and learn most effectively, and when, if you are having difficulty understanding something new, you automatically look for ways to process the new information using all your senses.

Sensory Learning Preferences:

The five senses through which we take information are: sight, sound, touch, taste and smell. These five senses create information stored in our brain using the same sensory systems – we can remember sights, sounds, sensations of touch, taste and smell. Have you ever noticed that you can also generate new thoughts in your mind using each of these sensory systems? And have you ever noticed that you have a preference for thinking using one sensory system over all the others?

These ways of representing information in your mind are often grouped into three main sensory styles called Visual – a preference for thinking in pictures; Auditory – a preference for thinking in sounds; and Kinesthetic – a preference for thinking using emotions, skin sensations or whole body experience. The idea of "learning styles" is the idea that if you organize your learning to suit your own thinking preferences you might be able to improve the effectiveness of your own learning.

You need to keep in mind, though, that no one person only learns only one way, every person can use all three sensory systems to learn but you may find that learning new material using one particular system – looking, listening or doing – sometimes works best for you. But also be aware that there are at least four different processes going on in your mind when you learn new things – how you take in information, how you process and understand it, how you store it and how you retrieve it later – and in each process, information can be represented in each of the three main sensory systems.

The most important thing to realize is that your mind is much more complex than any simple model of thinking and so the best thing *to always do* if you are having trouble learning something new, is simply try learning that thing all three ways:

- make sure you draw a picture, diagram or flowchart, or find a video to explain it AND

- try to explain it out loud to someone else or just to yourself, ask a friend or a teacher to explain it to you, or find a podcast on the topic AND

- make a model, or make up some flash-cards, a question-and-answer game or an experiment to make sense of it or to test yourself.

If you try learning things using all three sensory systems, you will find you will "get it" using a system that works well for you. But be aware that your best way of learning may be different for different subjects and also may be different for different types of information.

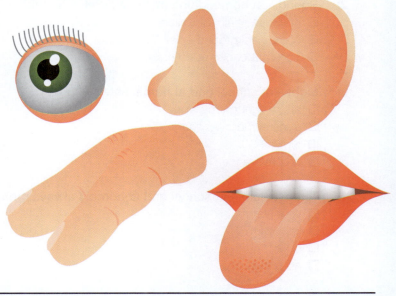

Exercise 1 – Examples of learning using the three sensory systems

a) Look at the table below and add in a few more examples of learning using each sensory system:

Visual: draw pictures, make idea maps, use color in notes, highlight key points
Auditory: read out loud, record and play back, teach someone else, have discussions and debates
Kinesthetic: use physical models, practicals, flash cards, play question-and-answer games

The best way of learning for all students is to try learning new things using all three ways – as something to see, something to hear and something to do.

b) Write down one visual, one auditory and one kinesthetic way of learning that you are prepared to try next time you are studying any topic in any subject you are finding is difficult to understand.

....

....

Make a commitment to try learning new or difficult material using all three sensory systems.

Exercise 2 – Environmental preferences

a) Think about learning new things at school or at home and ask yourself if any of the following factors are important for you.

Choose one or more things for each question:

1) **Sound – in class, I prefer things to be explained to me...**
   ☐ by the teacher
   ☐ by a classmate who understands it
   ☐ in a group by other students
   ☐ I don't like listening to others, I prefer to work things out by myself.

2) **Sound – at home, doing my homework, I prefer...**
   ☐ no noise at all, total silence
   ☐ some background noise like music
   ☐ constant background noise.

3) **Light – at school and at home, I always prefer...**
   ☐ bright light on my work
   ☐ general room lighting
   ☐ dim light
   ☐ no preference.

4) **Temperature – at school and at home, I always prefer the room to be...**
   ☐ very warm
   ☐ just warm
   ☐ cool
   ☐ no preference.

5) Setting – in class at school, I find I concentrate and learn best when...
- ☐ I am sitting with my friends
- ☐ I am not sitting with my friends but with other classmates
- ☐ I am sitting by myself.

6) Setting – at home, I like my work place to be...
- ☐ firm chair and desk
- ☐ soft chair and table
- ☐ on my bed
- ☐ on the floor.

7) Setting – in class, I find I concentrate best when I sit...
- ☐ at the front of the class
- ☐ near the windows
- ☐ away from the windows
- ☐ in the middle
- ☐ at the back of the class.

8) People – I prefer to do schoolwork...
- ☐ alone
- ☐ with a friend
- ☐ with an adult who can help me
- ☐ in a group.

9) Time of day – at school, my best time for concentration is...
- ☐ first thing in the morning
- ☐ just before lunch
- ☐ just after lunch
- ☐ in the afternoon.

10) Time of day – at home, I prefer getting my homework and study done...
- ☐ as soon as I arrive home from school
- ☐ after dinner
- ☐ late in the evening
- ☐ the next day, early before school starts.

b) putting all these environmental preferences together, what things could you do at home and at school to improve the effectiveness of your learning?

At school I could..

....

....

....

At home I could ....

....

....

....

Exercise 3 – Classroom learning

a) Think of two times at school recently when you learned something new, times when something suddenly made sense to you, when you "got it." And think of what was going on in the classroom at the time. How was the teacher teaching you – talking, pictures, data projected slides, videos, experiments, group work – and what were you doing – writing, drawing, discussing, listening?

Two times recently at school when I learned something well were...	What was going on in the classroom? How was the teacher teaching you and what were you doing?	Did anyone else help you to understand?

b) And then think of two times when you didn't learn well, what was going on then?

Two times recently at school when I didn't learn well were...	What was going on in the classroom? How was the teacher teaching you and what were you doing?	Why do you think you found it difficult to learn?

c) And now compare your positive and negative learning experiences and see if you can work out what factors seem to be most important for you when you are learning or trying to understand new things in the classroom.

I seem to learn best when ....

....

....

....

....

Using Technology

3j – Select and use technology effectively and productively.

6j – Understand and use technology systems.

Mastery

You will know you are at the **Expert** level in the use of this ATL skill set when you can automatically understand and use a collection of technologies – including libraries and different types of computers and communication systems – to find, process, store and communicate information.

Every day, you are surrounded by information technology (IT) systems which you use to collect, process, store and communicate information in order to investigate issues, situations and events, and learn to solve problems. IT systems are a combination of hardware and software (including apps), and the key for you to operate most effectively is to be able to identify and become comfortable using what is available to you to solve the problems you face in your everyday life – both in school and outside school. IT systems are simply tools. The effectiveness of any tool depends on the user.

Exercise 1 – Available technology

a) List the hardware and software available to you – both at school and at home – for each of the following purposes and rate your competence using each one as Low, Medium or High.

b) Highlight any from which you think you could benefit by becoming more competent with it.

Purpose	Hardware, software and apps	Rate your competence in using each one L M H
Research – finding information		
Information processing – developing understanding, making sense of information		
Information storage		
Communicating information – presentation systems		

c) Set yourself a goal to work on one technology system to improve your competence.

d) Do your research and find a person, a book or an on-line lesson on how to use the system.

My goal is to get better at using ....

I want to do this by ....

This will be useful to me for...

To learn how to get better with this I will use ....

Self-Assessment of ATL Skills

To see how best to use this page refer to pages 114 and 115.

ATL Skills	Novice *Watch*	Learner *Copy*	Practitioner *Do*				Expert *Share*
			Starting	*Practicing*	*Getting better*	*Got it!*	
Deadlines							
Exam Timetabling							
Achieving Goals							
Organize Equipment							
Organize Files							
Learning Preferences							
Use Technology							

Student Self-Assessment of ATL Skills Proficiency – ORGANIZATION SKILLS

AFFECTIVE SKILLS

A person's "affect" is the way that person expresses their emotions – the behaviors they use to demonstrate emotion. Great actors are very skilled in demonstrating the appropriate affect for different emotions displayed by the characters they are playing. The "affective domain," in educational terms, refers to how our feelings, values, enthusiasms, motivations, and attitudes affect our success in learning.

Learning new things when you are feeling positive and interested and you want to learn is easy, as I am sure you know. It is getting yourself to learn new things when you don't want to, when you are feeling demotivated and disinterested, that is hard. That's where the affective skills come in. Through practicing the skills in this cluster, you will learn how to concentrate well and overcome distractions. You will learn how to overcome procrastination and make yourself persevere with tasks until they are finished. You will also learn how to manage your emotions well, how to overcome feelings of stress and anxiety, how to deal with anger or any bullying and how to deal well with any failure to achieve your goals.

The last part of the affective skills is about learning how to be more resilient, or strong on the inside. Inner strength or mental toughness is a characteristic of all successful sports people, all great performers, business people, politicians, leaders in all areas, and it is a skill that anyone can develop.

GREAT RESILIENCE

In 1982 Mark Inglis, at the time a search-and-rescue mountaineer, and his partner, Philip Doole, were caught out on New Zealand's highest mountain, Mt. Cook, by an unexpected snow storm and had to dig a snow cave to survive. Unfortunately the blizzard lasted 13 days before they were rescued, and as a result, both men's legs were badly frost bitten and both Mark Inglis's legs had to be amputated below the knee. As a disabled athlete with two artificial limbs you might have thought his mountain-climbing days were over but in 2002 he returned to Mt. Cook and successfully climbed to the summit. Two years later, he successfully climbed Cho Oyu and on May 15, 2006, after 40 days of climbing, Inglis became the first ever double amputee to reach the summit of Mount Everest, the highest mountain in the world.

In addition to still climbing mountains, Mark Inglis is now a leukemia researcher, wine maker and motivational speaker, and provides an excellent role model and example of what can be achieved through perseverance, determination, self-motivation and resilience – all key affective skills.

Mindfulness

4.1a – Practice focus and concentration.
4.1b – Practice strategies to develop mental focus.
4.1c – Practice strategies to overcome distractions.
4.1d – Practice being aware of body-mind connections.

Mastery

You will know you are at the **Expert** level in the use of this ATL skill set when you are completely aware of your connection to the world around you through each of your senses and you are aware of your own thinking at any moment. When you are at the **Expert** level in this skill you will be able to use that awareness to manage your own thought processes, overcome any distractions and switch on a state of total focus and concentration, whenever you need to, in class or at home.

Your Senses:

All the information we get from the world comes to us through our five senses – sight, sound, touch, taste and smell. Every minute of every day we are getting lots of information through each of our senses but we usually only pay conscious attention to some of it. One aspect of developing mindfulness is learning to pay attention to all the information coming to us at any one moment.

Exercise 1 – Awareness of your senses

Take a moment to pause, sit quietly, go through your senses one at a time and notice all the things that you are aware of through each of your senses. Fill in the following table:

Some of the things I can see are:	
Some of the things I can hear are:	
Some of the smells I can notice are:	
What I can taste in my mouth is:	
What I can feel on my skin is:	
What I notice about my mood or my emotions right now is:	

Your thoughts:

Developing mindfulness also means becoming more aware of the thoughts that are going through your mind at any one moment. The two main ways in which we consciously think are in words and pictures. For example – right now as you read these words, do you notice what you are saying to yourself inside your head and what you are imagining? Do you notice that as you are reading the words I have written here you are probably saying these same words to yourself inside your head? That is a normal part of reading. Do these words also produce any pictures?

Exercise 2 – Your present thoughts

Take a moment to pause, sit quietly and close your eyes. Try not to think of anything in particular, just let your mind relax and notice your own thoughts. In particular notice what you say to yourself and what you imagine. After a minute or two, open your eyes and write down in the following table what you noticed about your own thinking.

What I said to myself was:	
What I pictured was:	

Distracting thoughts:

In class, we know we are concentrating when the thoughts inside our heads are focused on the same topic or ideas the teacher is talking about. We know we have lost concentration when we start thinking about other things. Do you notice the types of distracting thoughts that you tend to have most when you are supposed to be concentrating on what the teacher is saying or what you are studying or reading?

Exercise 3 – Distracting thoughts

Use the following table and pick the areas of thinking that you find distract you most when you are supposed to be concentrating – describe some examples of each one:

I get most distracted thinking about:	Some examples are:
People	
Places	
Things I have to do	
Things I would sooner be doing	
Memories	
Imagination	
Other examples?	

Exercise 4 – Practicing overcoming distracting thoughts

When you are in class and the teacher is explaining something to you, you can practice overcoming distracting thoughts by noticing every time your thoughts drift off to one of your usual distractions and deliberately practice bringing your thoughts back to what the teacher is talking about by:

a) repeating the words the teacher is using, to yourself, inside your head

b) thinking about what the teacher is saying and trying to predict what the teacher will say next

c) using your imagination to make pictures inside your head to represent what the teacher is talking about.

Concentration and distractions:

Have you ever noticed that you do concentrate really well, sometimes? And do you notice that when you are concentrating well you can absorb things really well, you can understand things really well and you can get 2-3 times as much work done in the same amount of time as you can when you are not concentrating well? So the first thing you need to do is to think of all the things you can set up that will help you to get into a state of high concentration. Every person is different. Every person has their own things that help them concentrate.

Exercise 5 – Controlling distractions – setting up your environment

Use the following table and fill in what works for you:

Environmental Factors	What helps you to concentrate the most:
Your study environment at home – desk, chair, lighting?	
Temperature – warm, hot, cool, cold?	
Time of day – before dawn, straight after school?	
Music – most people find that instrumental music helps concentration.	
Food?	
Rewards – things to look forward to?	
Other things?	

Exercise 6 – Controlling distractions – social media and the internet

When you are at home doing your homework or your study try this:

a) Set up your room with all the things from the previous exercise that you need to put in place to concentrate well.

b) Look at the clock – on the hour, set an alarm on your phone to ring in 45 minutes time.

c) Go to *Settings* on your phone, select *Airplane Mode* (what I call *Study Mode*).

d) Switch off all your social media platforms and chat apps.

e) Get into your work – focus on concentrating as well as you can.

f) When 45 minutes are up the alarm will ring.

g) Switch Study Mode off on your phone, open up all your social media platforms and check all your messages – **ONLY FOR 15 MINUTES!!**

h) Have the self-control you need to set yourself up on the hour again for 45 minutes of concentration followed by 15 minutes of checking your messages.

Monitoring your internal conversation:

What I am calling your *internal conversation* is simply what you say to yourself and what you imagine, inside your head. When you are in class and the teacher is teaching you things, try to build a habit of regularly checking how long you are staying focused on what the teacher is saying and how often you think of other things that distract your attention. Practice bringing yourself back to a state of concentration.

Exercise 7 – Concentrating in class

a) Practice repeating to yourself inside your head what the teacher just said – say the same words to yourself inside your head and you will pull yourself back and increase your concentration.

b) Anytime you notice you have drifted off from where your focus should be, try saying to yourself inside your head something like "I am here, now." Repeat this a couple of times and you will notice that your attention comes back to where your focus should be.

c) Try sitting quietly in a quiet place and just noticing your internal conversation. Don't try to control it or change it just "observe" it, notice what you are saying to yourself and what you are imaging inside your own head. Do this for 5 minutes per day and soon you will notice an improvement in your ability to stay focused and pay attention.

Exercise 8 – Practice mindfulness training

a) Physical relaxation – try sitting quietly. In a quiet room. In a comfortable chair and closing your eyes. Focus on one part of your body at a time, starting with your toes on one foot. First tighten up all the muscles in that part of your body. Hold that tension for a count of 10 and then relax that part of your body completely. Feel all the tension drain away from that part of your body then move to the next part – the whole of your foot – and repeat the same tension/relaxation exercise. Then move your attention to your calf muscles, then your knee muscles, then the toes on the other foot, etc. right up your whole body, with all your attention on one part of your body at a time, slowly moving up until you have relaxed the whole of your physical body. Notice if there are any parts of your body that are harder to relax than others, take longer with those parts, repeat the tension/relaxation several times until you feel that part is properly relaxed.

b) Simple meditation can have a big effect on your ability to focus, concentrate and become more aware. Once a day, maybe in the early morning or evening, take a 20-30 minute break to sit quietly, close your eyes and focus simply on your breathing. Try to stay focused on your breathing and allow any other thoughts to just pass through your mind, noticed but allowed to float away. The more you do this exercise the easier it will become and the easier you will find it to produce a state of concentration when you need it.

Perseverance

4.2a – Demonstrate persistence and perseverance.
4.2b – Practice delaying gratification.

Mastery

You will know you are at the **Expert** level in the use of this 21st C skill when you can get yourself to start your own work when you need to (even when you don't want to) and stick at one task for an extended period of time or until it is completed.

Learning how to persevere is partly about learning how to overcome distractions and concentrate well (see ***4.1a,b,c,d – Mindfulness***) partly about how to motivate yourself (see ***4.4a,b,c – Self-motivation***) and partly about learning how to overcome procrastination and get yourself to "stick at it," whatever "it" may be. First you need to practice all the concentration, motivation and self-talk exercises and then try the following exercises.

Exercise 1 – How do you do it now?

Do you notice that sometimes you do manage to persist and to persevere with tasks? You work hard at them and you don't give up until you have finished? How do you get yourself to do that sometimes?

a) Remember a time when you did persevere and completed a task, some homework, an assignment. A time when you started the task when you needed to and you kept on working until you finished.

b) Close your eyes, remember that incident in detail, what happened before, during and after that time. Notice what was going on in your mind at the time when you were persevering well, what were you saying to yourself, what were you imagining, what else was going on?

c) Open your eyes and write all those things down now. Describe the experience clearly, precisely and analytically.................

....

....

d) What are two key things that you seem to need to do in order to persevere with something?

1. ....

2. ....

e) What if it was something you didn't want to do or you didn't like to do; What could you do then?.......................

....

....

....

f) What do your friends do? Talk to someone else, look at what they wrote, find something that someone else does that you could try for yourself? Write it here – something I could try, to help me persevere is:

....

....

....

The more you practice it the better you will become until you get so good you can switch on perseverance whenever you need it.

Exercise 2 – Overcoming procrastination

The first thing you need to realize is that everyone procrastinates – everyone. Procrastination is the single biggest reason why people don't achieve their goals so it is the most important thing for you to learn to avoid in order to be successful, whatever you imagine success to be. Overcoming procrastination is not a simple thing. It is made up of several different strategies, but you can do it because you already do – sometimes. The trick is how to get yourself to do it deliberately, every time you need to.

a) When you have serious schoolwork to do, do you ever find that suddenly you seem to find a whole lot of chores that need doing that you do instead of getting started? Write here all the things you do, like cleaning, tidying, exercising, etc., that delay you in getting started on your work.

   ....

   ....

b) When you have serious schoolwork to do, do you also notice that you give yourself excuses or reasons why you don't need to get on with it right now? Write here all the reasons you give yourself, like "I can do it at first break tomorrow," "I need to wait until I am in a more creative frame of mind," etc., that you use to delay starting the work you need to do.

   ....

   ....

c) Write here all the things you use, like social media and computer games, to distract yourself from thinking about the tasks you need to get done.

   ....

   ....

Exercise 3 – Creating urgency

Have you ever noticed that sometimes you do manage to overcome procrastination quite successfully? Usually when something is "due in tomorrow" right? Because you use that external motivator (avoiding getting into trouble for late work) to create a sense of urgency within you. Do you think you could generate the same sense of urgency within yourself on purpose, without the teacher having to do it for you? It might be useful for you to first work through the assignment timetabling exercise (**3a – Plan short-term and long-term assignments; meet deadlines** on page 70) and the exercises on goals (**3d – Set goals that are challenging and realistic** on page 70 and **3e – Plan strategies and take action to achieve personal and academic goals** on page 74). Then use the following exercise to create a sense of urgency to get the work done:

a) Pick a task that you need to get done now that you have been putting off doing.

   The task is..

b) What are some examples of things you could say to yourself that would support your best efforts but would also create a sense of urgency to get you started on some work you know you need to do?

   ....

   ....

c) What might be the worst possible consequences of not getting this task done?

   ....

   ....

d) What might be the best possible consequences of getting this task done now?

   ....

   ....

Make sure you have the reward AFTER you finish the work not before you start, or halfway through.

Exercise 4 – Reflection on perseverance

What are the things that help most, the things hinder most and the actions you could take?

Fill in the following table:

Five things that help me most to get things started and completed are:	Five things that most get in the way of me getting things started and completed are:	One thing I could do for each that would help me to persevere in starting and completing tasks:
1.		
2.		
3.		
4.		
5.		

Impulsiveness and Anger

4.3a – Practice strategies to overcome impulsiveness and anger.

Mastery

You will know you are at the **Expert** level in the use of this ATL skill set when you automatically take charge of the way you are thinking to manage any impulsiveness, you recognize when your emotions are beginning to intensify into anger and you use self-calming strategies.

When you jump the gun without thinking about what you are going to do, you are not in charge of yourself. The old saying about counting to ten before you speak and act is one sure way to overcome impulsivity and there are many other effective strategies as well.

Unless you are being bullied, no one else makes you angry except yourself. Anger occurs when your emotions intensify to a level where you find them difficult to control. The key is to raise your awareness of your emotions and have coping strategies in place to calm yourself.

Anger. Getting angry is usually the end of a process which starts with mild irritation. People are very different in how they react to situations. Some people are very fast to anger, some are very slow. If you can start to notice the signals that as you move from irritation to anger, then you can learn how to easily control any anger.

Exercise 1 – Noticing the signals

a) When you get a bit irritated with someone or something and it starts building up into anger, what do you notice happening in your body? Is your breathing getting faster or slower? Is your heart rate getting faster or slower? Are your relaxed or tense? Where in your body are you most relaxed? Where are you the most tense?

....

....

....

b) When you get a bit irritated with someone or something and it starts building up into anger, what do you notice happening in your mind? What are you probably saying to yourself? What might you be imagining? How do you feel, physically and emotionally?

....

....

....

c) Ask two friends to describe what you look like on the outside when you begin to become angry. What is your face like? How do you hold your body? What is your voice like?

....

....

....

d) Draw an outline of your body on a big piece of paper:

i.   On the inside of the outline write in red the things you notice about yourself when you begin to become angry on the parts of your body where you feel them

ii. On the outside of the outline write in blue the things your friends notice about you when you begin to become angry on the parts of your body where you feel them.

Self-calming. Once you have started to recognize the signals that lead you to anger, you will need to learn how to calm yourself down to prevent irritation turning into anger. There are four key ways that most people use.

Exercise 2 – Practice these self-calming exercises when you are not angry so that you will be familiar with how to use them when you need to.

1) Count your breaths – focus on your breathing, say to yourself *breathe in, breathe out* in a nice steady rhythm. Count each breath. Try to slow down both the count and your breathing.

2) Tense and release – notice which parts of your body are most tensed up and clench them really tight and then release them completely. Move that tense/relax reaction all over your body.

3) Stretch and release – stretch upwards and outwards as much as you can and then release

4) Be here, now – say to yourself *I am here, now* and focus on your senses, noticing what you can see, hear, taste, smell and feel on your skin.

Impulsiveness. Impulsiveness is when you speak or act without thinking – sometimes with disastrous results. You are impulsive when you are not well connected to the moment at hand and what is going on around you.

Exercise 3

a) With a partner discuss one time when each of you have done something without thinking, that, on reflection, you wish you hadn't done. What happened?

....

....

b) Now think about the consequences of your actions. How did it affect other people? How do you think they felt at the time?

....

....

c) Think about other people in the class and write down five times you have seen someone else act impulsively with a bad result, and how that affected other people:

What happened was:	How that affected other people was:
1.	
2.	
3.	
4.	
5.	

d) What do all these instances of impulsivity have in common? Can you think of two or three things?

....

....

e) In each case what could the person have done differently to achieve a better outcome?

1. ....

2. ....

3. ....

4. ....

5. ....

f) Work together with your partner and come up with two or three key things that you are going to do to manage your own impulsiveness from now on.

....

....

Bullying

4.3b – Practice strategies to prevent and eliminate bullying.

Mastery

You will know you are at the **Expert** level in the use of this ATL skill when you can automatically recognize when bullying is occurring and implement strategies to prevent and eliminate it.

Bullying is a severe form of harassment which cannot be tolerated in any community. Everyone has the right to feel good about themselves, and bullying must be addressed immediately to protect this right – it won't just go away by itself. Bullying is when one person uses their power over someone else to make them feel helpless, powerless and anxious. Bullying can be of a physical, mental or emotional kind – it can be expressed by physical actions, spoken words or written words or images.

STOP BULLYING!

Exercise 1 – Recognizing bullying

a) With a partner, brainstorm different ways people can bully others. For example, electronic messaging ....
....
....
....

b) Discuss with a partner times you both have been bullied, seen others bullied or been a bully yourselves and describe the emotions you felt.

c) Then describe what you thought later on that you should have done or could have done differently.

	How I felt was ...	What I could have done differently was ...
A time I was bullied was ...		
A time I saw someone else bullied was ...		
A time when I bullied someone else was ...		

d) Discuss with your partner, do some research and come up with what you think are the most important things you could do in the future if you find yourself being bullied.

Type of bullying	What to do
Physical bullying – someone pushing you around, trying to hurt you.	
Emotional bullying – someone trying to make you feel bad, blaming you, putting you down.	
Intellectual bullying – someone telling you that you are stupid, dumb, not capable.	
Cyber bullying – someone using text messages or social media to insult you or say bad things about you.	

e) It might be useful to work your way through **1.1h – Participate in, and contribute to, digital social media networks** and **2a – Use social media networks appropriately to build and develop relationships** on page 16 to help you understand how to stay safe on-line and not leave yourself open to cyber bullying.

Exercise 2 – Dealing with bullying

Your class has been given an assignment to write a new bullying policy for your school.
Work in pairs or in a small group.

a) Make sure you define clearly what is bullying and what is just bad behavior – they are not the same.

Bullying is ....

....

....

Bullying is not ....

....

....

b) Work your way through all the points in the following table:

Types of bullying	What students can do		What teachers can do		What schools can do	
	When it happens	To prevent it happening again in the future	When it happens	To prevent it happening again in the future	When it happens	To prevent it happening again in the future
Physical bullying						
Emotional bullying						
Mental bullying						
Cyber bullying						

c) Work out a simple system that you could set up at school for anyone to use to report bullying. Would you want it to be anonymous? Confidential?

d) Next come up with a process to investigate and take action on any reports of bullying.

e) Come up with an overall policy statement that would sum up the school's attitude towards any types of bullying in the future.

At this school...

....

....

Pressure and Stress

4.3c – Practice strategies to reduce stress and anxiety.

Mastery

You will know you are at the **Expert** level in the use of this ATL skill when you can deliberately reduce the feelings of stress and anxiety that sometimes beset you and get yourself back to a stable, calm, effective state of mind any time you need to.

In Physics terms, pressure is the force applied to an object, stress is deformity under pressure. We all have pressures being applied to us all the time. Pressure can be a very useful and positive thing – we can use pressure to get a lot of things done when they need to be done. It is when pressure turns into stress that our effectiveness and our efficiency reduces severely and we risk doing ourselves emotional and mental harm. Learning how to deal well with pressure and eliminate stress are critical skills in today's high-expectation school environment.

Exercise 1 – Handling pressure

a) Make a list of all the pressures on you that you notice on a daily basis at school, and where each pressure comes from.

_____

_____

_____

_____

_____

_____

_____

b) Dealing well with pressures is partly time management, partly motivation and partly managing self-talk.

It might be useful for you to do all the exercises from *3a – Plan short-term and long-term assignments, meet deadlines; 3c – Keep and use a weekly planner for assignments;* and *3d – Set goals that are challenging and realistic* on page 70, as well as *3e – Plan strategies and take action to achieve personal and academic goals* on page 74. Also *4.4a – Practice analyzing and attributing causes for success and failure; 4.4b – Practice managing self-talk;* and *4.4c – Practice positive thinking* on page 101.

Exercise 2 – How do you do it now?

Do you notice that sometimes you do manage to deal well with stress and overcome anxieties? Sometimes you have managed to get past these things and back into a better frame of mind? How do you make yourself do that sometimes?

i. remember a time when you did manage to deal well with stress and/or anxiety and you were able to get back into a more positive and more effective frame of mind

ii. close your eyes, remember that incident in detail, what happened before that moment, during that moment and after that moment – what can you see … hear … how did it feel?

iii. notice what was going on in your mind at the time you were managing stress and/or anxiety well, what were you saying to yourself, what were you imagining, what else was going on?

iv. Open your eyes and write all those things down. Describe the experience clearly, precisely and analytically.

_____

_____

_____

v. Label what you have written down as your own Stress Reduction Strategy .

vi. Now that you know how you have done it sometimes, practice doing all those same things deliberately when next you need to exercise that skill

vii. The more you practice it the better you will become until you get so good at it you can switch on stress reduction whenever you need it.

Exercise 3 – Exercises to reduce stress and anxiety

a) Learning to physically relax can be a big help in achieving mental relaxation and overcoming stress and anxiety – see **4.1 Mindfulness** exercises on page 86.

b) Rhythmic physical movement and stretching, such as are involved in walking, jogging, dancing, yoga, tai-chi and some martial arts, can be very useful in helping to reduce the effects of stress and anxiety.

c) Humor, especially the type of humor that causes you to laugh out loud, can be very useful in reducing the effects of stress and anxiety.

d) Music can help, especially relaxing music or music which gets you up and dancing. Make up one playlist for relaxing and another playlist for energetic dancing – both can help reduce stress and anxiety.

e) Visualization can also be used to develop the ability to overcome anxiety and stress reactions by deliberately generating a calm, relaxed, focused and confident state of mind.

This is a visualization exercise to help you set up a kind of "switch" in your body that you will be able to use to "switch on" a feeling of calmness, of relaxed, focused attention which will enable you to instantly overcome any feelings of anxiety or stress and enable you to focus on what you need to do instead. This exercise requires you to imagine something, preferably with your eyes shut. Which means it is going to be hard to read what to do and to do the exercise at the same time.

What I suggest you do is read through the whole of the exercise so you know what to do, then get someone else to talk you through the visualization the first time – with them reading the script out loud.

In order to get this technique to work, you will need to practice it once a day for a while but after you have done it once with someone else's help, you should be able to generate the visualization yourself without outside help.

To do this you need to set up two things first:

1) You need to think of a time from your own life when you were feeling calm, relaxed, focused and quietly confident that you could achieve what you needed to do. When you were playing your favorite game or in your best class or reading a book, playing a musical instrument or riding your skateboard – anytime when you were doing anything at all that you enjoy and feel confident that you can do reasonably well. Think of a time from your own life that you could use. Remember where you were and what was happening at the time.

2) A unique physical action we can use as a link for you to be able to switch this feeling on when you need it. The physical action that I want you to use is a clenched fist, in a grab action pulled back towards yourself like you might do if you were celebrating a great success. This is like a symbol of success anyway.

So, when you do the visualization and you generate the feeling of calm, relaxed, focused confidence coming up inside you, you are going to capture it in a clenched fist.

Once you have practiced this same action once a day for about 3 weeks, you will have established the link in your brain between the neurons which control the clenched fist and the neurons which generate that feeling of confidence.

Once that link is established, anytime you need to feel confident all you will have to do is clench your fist in the same way, and you will re-generate that same feeling of confidence straight away!

And because you can't feel anxious or stressed and confident at the same time, your nervousness will disappear and you will be able to concentrate well and do the work that you need to do to achieve your goal.

So, set up someone to read through the script here and all you have to do is relax, maybe put your head down on your desk, and close your eyes – just relax and be still.

[reading out loud, in a calm, quiet voice, really, really slowly, pausing at the dots ...]

First I just want you to relax.

Breathe deeply and relax your back, relax your neck, just relax.

Now that you are feeling really relaxed what I want you to do is imagine something.

I want you to imagine a big screen TV in your mind, a big blank screen in your mind, nothing on the screen at present ... and up on that screen I want you to bring up an image of you in that moment when you were feeling calm, relaxed, focused and quietly confident ... remember where you were, who else was there, what was going on at the time and see yourself clearly on the screen in that moment and just freeze that image for a moment ... notice the colors that you can see on that screen in your mind ... and take your color control and brighten up all the colors, make them really bright and clear just for a moment ... and now bring the sound up too and notice the sounds that you could hear in that moment when you were feeling so calm and relaxed, focused and confident. Notice what you could hear ... and now notice what you were saying to yourself when you were feeling so calm and confident. Hear those words now ... and now I want you to imagine you are moving closer to that TV screen in your mind, and closer, until you are so close you can step right into that picture and be there now ... and release the freeze frame and go through the moment and notice what it feels like to feel calm and relaxed, focused and confident ... and when you notice those feelings, when you start to feel that great feeling of calmness and confidence coming up inside you, I want you to take one of your hands and clench it tight into a fist ... do that now and lock in that feeling ... kind of hold onto that feeling with a clenched fist, do it now ... (long pause) ... and then open your hand again and relax your fingers again and open your eyes and come back to now.

[brisk, sharp voice]

welcome back!

Now I have shown you what to do. If you want it to work for you, you have to practice – once a day for about three weeks. The steps are:

i. remember a time when you were feeling calm, relaxed and quietly confident- see it, hear it and feel it

ii. lock in the feeling with a clenched fist

iii. practice once a day for 21 days.

When you have done that, you will have built up a trigger or a switch in your brain that you can use whenever you need to, to switch on a feeling of calm, relaxed, focused confidence –

iv. so, anytime you notice you have started to feel overwhelmed, or stressed or anxious about your schoolwork, or your deadlines, or your tests or exams, all you have to do is fire off your trigger – clench that fist – and you will recreate that calm confident feeling throughout your body, your anxiety and feelings of stress will disappear and you will be able to apply the whole of your brain to what you need to do.

Self-Motivation

4.4a – Practice analyzing and attributing causes for success and failure.
4.4b – Practice managing self-talk.
4.4c – Practice positive thinking.

Mastery

You will know you are at the **Expert** level in the use of this ATL skill set when you can get yourself to actively and positively do things that you really don't want to do.

Exercise 1 – Purpose

Do you want to succeed at school? If so why? What are your most important reasons?

a) Put the following twelve ideas into a priority list. Which is first – most important to you – which is second and so on. Write one number from 1-12 next to each point.

- [ ] to get a good job – earn serious money?
- [ ] to feel satisfied, proud of yourself?
- [ ] to get into the right university?
- [ ] to get a feel for your progress to date?
- [ ] because your parents want you to?
- [ ] to test yourself and see what you are capable of?
- [ ] to prove how smart you are?
- [ ] to gain knowledge and skills that will be useful to you in your life?
- [ ] to be better able to mix with other smart kids?
- [ ] to develop your intelligence?
- [ ] to make your parents proud?
- [ ] to practice concentration, determination and the exercise of effort?

Your reasons for wanting to succeed have an influence on your motivation, especially when times get tough. Within this list there are two types of factors and each type has a different influence on motivation.

The two types of reasons are:

i. those that stem from intrinsic motivators:
   - to feel satisfied, proud of yourself
   - to get a feel for your progress to date
   - to test yourself and see what you are capable of
   - to gain knowledge and skills that will be useful to you in your life
   - to develop your intelligence
   - to practice concentration, determination and the exercise of effort

ii. and those that stem from extrinsic motivators:
   - to get a good job – earn serious money
   - to get into the right university
   - because your parents want you to
   - to prove how smart you are
   - to be able to mix with other smart kids
   - to make your parents proud.

Extrinsic motivators are very important particularly in helping us turn ideas and ambitions into goals, but research shows that, of the two, **intrinsic motivators are the more powerful.**

The reason being that intrinsic motivators are things that are in your control whereas extrinsic motivators are out of your control.

When times get hard, when you get to the point where you feel like you have had enough and you just want to stop, it is the intrinsic motivators, a sense of pride, a feeling of capability, that are the most powerful in helping you get over the hump and keep going until the job is finished.

Use your external motivators to help you dream and create long-term plans – but cement those long-term plans with internal motivators to get you through the hard work facing you now.

Definitions:

 Success – when you set a goal and you do achieve it.

 Failure – when you set a goal and don't achieve it.

Self-motivation has a lot to do with what is called "Attribution." What that means is – what do you see as the causes of any success or failure that you have?

Exercise 2 – Success and failure

a) Think of a time when you had a success, any success, any time that you set a goal and achieved it. It can be any sort of success – a time when you got the grade, the mark or the performance that you wanted, a time when your team won a game, or you remembered your lines in the play, or you danced well, sang well, got out of bed on time – any time at all when you achieved the outcome you wanted.

b) Then think of a time when you had a failure, any failure, any time when you set a goal and didn't achieve it – any time when you didn't achieve the outcome you wanted.

c) Now write in what you see as the reasons for your success and your failure.

	What happened?	What were the causes of your success and failure?
One time when I had a success – I set a goal and achieved it.		
One time when I had a failure – I set a goal and didn't achieve it.		

There are two different types of factors you could have written down as the causes of your success and failure:

Those that are in your control	*Those that are out of your control*
<ul><li>How much effort you put in?</li><li>Your time management strategies?</li><li>Your learning strategies?</li><li>Your concentration and focus?</li><li>How you deal with any setbacks or failures?</li></ul> 	<ul><li>Your teachers</li><li>Your school</li><li>Your parents</li><li>Luck</li><li>Weather</li><li>Fate</li></ul> 

Self-motivation has a lot to do with focusing on the things that are in your control as the reasons for any success or failure. If you make sure you always focus on what is in your control, then you can always do something about creating more success for yourself and dealing well with any failures.

d) To practice strategies to give you more control over your own learning and more success in learning all your subjects work through *Exercises 3i – Understand and use sensory learning preferences* on page 79.

Self-talk

Do you notice that sometimes you talk to yourself inside your head? That is called your self-talk or your internal dialogue. Everyone talks to themselves, it's normal, and everyone talks to themselves both positively and negatively. The trick with managing your self-talk is to manage your perspective – the aspect of your self-talk on which you choose to focus. Focus on the positives and deal with the negatives while making sure you are always true to yourself – never trying to lie to yourself or fool yourself. Learning to manage what you say to yourself inside your own mind is an important step in generating self-motivation (also see **Exercise 4.1c – Practice strategies to overcome distractions** on page 86).

Exercise 3 – Managing self-talk

Try these strategies, repeat them, practice them until they become habits:

a) Notice any self-sabotage and don't let it occupy your thoughts. Practice changing your perspective, your focus, by changing your language – what you say to yourself:

i. Instead of focusing on past mistakes or possible future mistakes – focus on what is happening right now, in the present:

What could you say to yourself to get you to focus on the present, on what is happening at that moment?

....

....

ii. Instead of focusing on weaknesses – what you are not so good at – focus on your strengths – the things you feel you are good at:

Write down two things that you do well.

....

....

iii. Instead of focusing on outcome – end result – focus on the process with which you are engaged, and make sure you enjoy what you are doing right now to achieve that outcome:

What are you doing right now that you enjoy doing, that you put effort into?

....

....

iv. Instead of focusing on things you can't control like the weather or luck or fate or teachers – focus on the things you can control:

What are some of the things that you can control that have an effect on your learning and understanding at school?

....

....

v. Instead of focusing on perfection – nothing is ever perfect – focus on doing the best you can:

What could you say to yourself to get yourself to do the very best you can?

....

....

....

....

....

....

b) Notice any negative thoughts, interrupt them and deliberately change them.

   i.   First notice any negative thoughts:

Write down three negative things that you sometimes say to yourself, e.g. *I am no good at this, I can't do this?*

....

....

   ii. As soon as you notice those thoughts interrupt them – in your mind, in a loud (internal) voice say STOP! You might also like to imagine a big red STOP sign in your mind – sounds silly but it does help.

   iii. Then replace those thoughts by deliberately saying to yourself something like "I can handle this today", "I can get through this today," "I can do this today," "I am bigger than this," "I am stronger than this" – focus on the possible.

Choose one and write it here or make up one of your own.

....

....

....

   iv. Practice doing this over and over until it becomes second nature and you just do it automatically.

c) Use visualisation to focus your thoughts on the process, on the present:

   i.   Before you start the piece of work or the test or the performance, imagine yourself in the process, doing it and doing it well

   ii. Imagine yourself maximizing your effort, pushing yourself to your best performance, using the best strategies, the smartest techniques

   iii. Talk to yourself about where you focus will be when you are doing it, your concentration, your focus, your technique, and how you are going to do it well.

d) Avoid creating any negative prophecy. Think of anything that you have ever said to yourself about yourself that involves the words "I can't" – like "I can't sing," "I can't draw," "I can't do math," and notice how that language creates a negative prediction of your own future. When you say "I can't," what you mean is "this thing is impossible for me," "I don't have the ability," "I never ever will" but you don't know that for sure do you? Maybe sometime in your life you might learn how to do that thing, you might have a go at it, you might succeed at that thing – surely it is possible? To make sure you hold that possibility open, what you need to do is to:

   i.   Turn every "I can't" into an "I haven't yet" – because that is the simple truth, isn't it? If you turn every "I can't" in your life into an "I haven't yet," everything becomes possible for you.

Positive Thinking

Positive thinking doesn't mean fooling yourself, it doesn't mean being unrealistic, it just means adjusting your perspective so that you build a habit of focusing on the positives aspects of your life and the life around you.

Exercise 4 – Practice positive thinking

i. Write down a list of successes you have had in your life – any times at all that you have achieved what you have wanted to achieve – big successes or small successes.

....

....

....

....

ii. Write down a second list, this time of all the positive features of your daily life, the things that many people in the world don't have that you tend to take for granted, things for which you could be grateful – things like having a roof over your head at night, food on the table, people who care for you, a good education, etc.

....

....

....

....

Copy these two lists out on nice paper and pin them on a wall somewhere, maybe in your bedroom. Read over them every day and see if you can add to each one frequently:

iii. Commit random acts of spontaneous kindness – help someone out who is less fortunate than you, or someone who is having difficulty with something.

Think of one person you could help in some way. Describe what you could do:

....

....

iv. Challenge yourself always to take the action you need to take to achieve your goals.

Name three goals you have for this year and describe one thing you are doing to help you achieve each one.

Goal	Action I am taking
1.	
2.	
3.	

v. Celebrate all your successes and any good luck

How do you most like to celebrate? Name three things that you like to give yourself as rewards:

....

....

....

vi. Continuously make and update positive future plans

Name one thing that you would most like to be doing in 5 years' time: ....

Name one thing that you would most like to be doing in 10 years' time: ....

Name one thing that you would most like to be doing in 20 years' time: ....

vii. Encourage your friends and others around you to be more positive and to help others

Think of someone you know who could do with some encouragement to see the world in a more positive light. Don't name them, but write down what you could do to help them to think more positively.

....

....

Exercise 5 – How do you do it now?

a) Remember a time when you did motivate yourself to do something that you didn't particularly want to do but you needed to do, and you managed to get it done – whatever it was.

b) Close your eyes, remember that incident in detail – what happened before, during and after that time. Notice what was going on in your mind at the time when you felt motivated – what were you saying to yourself, what were you imagining, what else was going on?

c) Open your eyes and write all those things down now, describe the experience clearly, precisely and analytically.

....

....

d) What are two key things that you seem to need to do in order to feel motivated?

1. ....

2. ....

e) What if it was something you really, really didn't want to do or didn't like to do, What could you do then?

....

....

f) What do your friends do? Talk to someone else, look at what they wrote, find something that someone else does that you could try for yourself? Write it here:

Something I could try, to help me be more self-motivated is:

....

....

The more you practice it the better you will become until you get so good at it you can switch on self-motivation whenever you need it.

Resilience

4.5a – Practice "bouncing back" after adversity, mistakes and failure.
4.5c – Practice dealing with disappointment and unmet expectations.
4.5d – Practice dealing with change.

Mastery

You will know you are at the **Expert** level in the use of this ATL skill set when you cope well with any adversity or change in your life and "bounce back" quickly to full performance again.

Resilience is a multi-faceted concept and includes elements of many other Affective skills. In order to practice this skill, it would probably be useful if you first worked through all the exercises around successfully setting and achieving goals (*3d – Set goals that are challenging and realistic* on page 70, and *3e – Plan strategies and take action to achieve personal and academic goals* on page 74) and then all the Self-Motivation skills exercises on page 101 (*4.4a – Practice analyzing and attributing causes for success and failure, 4.4b – Practice managing self-talk* and *4.4c – Practice positive thinking*) and finally the exercise where you learn how to deal well with failure (*4.5b – Practice "failing well"* on page 109).

RESILIENCE – Resilient Learners have the following characteristics:

	Resilient students	Vulnerable students
Goals	Set learning goals – learn in order to understand.	Set performance goals – learn only in order to get the best grade.
Tasks	Take on new tasks to test themselves, to work towards mastery.	Take on new tasks to gain approval or avoid disapproval.
Challenge	Actively seek out new challenges.	Avoid all new challenges.
To achieve success	Believe effort is more important than ability.	Believe ability is more important than effort.
Reaction to failure	Fail Well – take responsibility, analyze the process, make changes, have another go. Do not have an emotional reaction to failure, realize that dealing well with failure is an important part of generating success.	Fail Badly – take no responsibility, blame others or the 'system,' repeat the same process or do even less, give up. Have major emotional reactions to failure.
Reaction to success	Think they can generate their own success.	Think that any success they have is due to the actions of other people.
View of Intelligence	Believe their intelligence is flexible, can be developed and increased.	Believe their intelligence is fixed, unalterable with a definite limit.
Performance	High achievers.	Under achievers.
Future Expectations	Optimistic.	Pessimistic.

Exercise 1 – To develop more resilience

1) Learn for understanding, not for a particular test. Developing understanding will produce more effective learning and better memory. Look for any gaps in your own understanding and ask questions to fill any gaps you identify (work through *5e – Consider content* on page 116).

2) Focus on the skills of effective learning. Learn how to concentrate well, motivate yourself when you need to and how to get organized, set goals and achieve them. These are the key skills of effective learners (work through *3a – Plan short-term and long-term assignments* and *3c – Keep and use a weekly planner for assignments* on page 70; *3b – Create plans to prepare for summative assessments* on page 72; *4.1a – Practice focus and concentration, 4.1b – Practice strategies to develop mental focus* and *4.1c – Practice strategies to overcome distractions* on page 86; and *4.2a – Demonstrate persistence and perseverance* and *4.2b – Practice delaying gratification* on page 90).

3) Set high standards for yourself and push yourself to achieve them.

4) Learn how to "fail well." Overcome any emotional reaction to failure, use any failure as good feedback, work out what you did wrong, make changes and go back and do it again, but do it differently the second time around.

5) Realize that your intelligence is flexible, multi-faceted and open to change, development and improvement. Eliminate any ideas of intelligence as something that is fixed and rigid.

6) Focus any learning failure on the things over which you have control – the amount of effort you put in and what strategies you use. Make sure you have a wide range of learning strategies you can employ in learning any new material in your subject (work through *3i – Understand and use sensory learning preferences (learning styles); 5c – Demonstrate flexibility in the selection and use of learning strategies; 5a – Develop new skills, techniques and strategies for effective learning, 5b – Identify strengths and weaknesses of personal learning strategies (self-assessment)* and *5g – Consider personal learning strategies* on page 79).

7) Constantly develop and update your own positive future plans.

Exercise 2 – Practice "bouncing back"

a) Working with a partner or a friend, write down one example of a time when you were working on a task, doing a job, playing a game, or trying to learn something new and you suffered a disappointment or a set-back or a problem. But it needs to be a time when you did manage to get back up again and finish off the task, the job, the game, the learning.

b) Write down some details of what happened.

c) Now close your eyes and try to remember the exact moment when you "bounced back." In as much detail as possible, think about what happened before, during and after that moment – what could you see...hear...how did it feel?

d) Notice what was going on in your mind at the time when you managed to bounce back – what were you saying to yourself, what were you imagining, what else was going on?

e) Open your eyes and write all those things down. Describe the experience clearly, precisely and analytically.

f) Label what you have written down as your own Resilience Strategy.

MY RESILIENCE STRATEGY

....

....

....

....

....

g) Now that you know how you have made yourself do it at times, practice doing all those same things deliberately when next you need to exercise that skill.

h) The more you practice it, the better you will become, until you get so good at it, you can switch on resilience whenever you need it.

Failing Well

4.5b – Practice "failing well."

Mastery

You will know you are at the **Expert** level in the use of this ATL skill when failing to achieve any goal causes you to automatically review your performance, make changes to your process and try again, and keep doing so until you achieve the goal.

Resilience is a multi-faceted concept and includes elements of many other Affective skills. In order to practice this skill it would probably be useful if you first worked through all the Self-Motivation skills exercises (**4.4a Practice analyzing and attributing causes for success and failure, 4.4b Practice managing self-talk** and **4.4c Practice positive thinking**).

Definitions:
Success is when you set a goal and you achieve it.
Failure is when you set a goal and you don't achieve it.

Exercise 1 – Learning to fail well using past experience

a) Think of any goal you have set in the past and not achieved. Any goal, big or small is OK but it needs to be something you would still like to achieve now.

b) Describe what the goal was – clearly and specifically.

....

....

c) Describe what action you took to achieve that goal – what did you do?

....

....

d) Describe what the result was, sticking only to the facts. List the facts clearly and precisely.

....

....

....

e) Analyze the process you used to achieve your goal and identify the factors that were in your control and those that were not in your control. Make two lists:

1. The factors that were in my control were ....

....

2. The factors that were not in my control were ....

....

f) Looking only at the factors that were in your control and the actions you took to achieve your goal, consider which of your actions worked well – helped you to move closer to your goal – and which of your actions didn't work – did not move you closer to achieving your goal. Make two lists:

1. The things I did that worked were...

....

2. The things I did that didn't work were..

....

g) Looking at the things you did last time that didn't work, make a plan to do one or more of those things differently next time. Describe what changes you are going to make to your process – what are you are going to do differently the second time around?

....

....

h) Take action again, make those changes, approach the same goal using a different process.

i) Go back to 1d and repeat the process again.

j) Keep repeating the process until you achieve your goal.

Exercise 2 – Using failing well to help you achieve a new goal

a) Think of a new goal you would like to achieve – any goal, big or small is OK.

b) Start at the top of the first column describing your goal clearly. Then work your way down the first column filling in the boxes as you go. This process will probably take some time, maybe weeks to complete, as you work your way through the actions you need to take to achieve your goal.

c) When you get to the bottom of the first column, move to the top of the second column and write in your new goal (it may be the same as the first goal, or you may have modified it based on your experience).

d) Then describe the action you are going to take, what you are going to do differently this time around.

e) Take that action and work subsequently down the second column.

f) Repeat, and repeat until you achieve your goal.

	My goal is...	My subsequent goal?
What action will you take, exactly what are you going to do to achieve that goal?	I will...	I will...
What was the result? Describe what happened clearly and precisely – list the facts.	What happened was...	What happened was...

What actions worked?	What I did that worked was...	What I did that worked was...
What didn't work?	What I did that didn't worked was...	What I did that didn't worked was...
What will you change?	What I will do differently next time is...	What I will do differently next time is...

Exercise 3 – Using failing well for academic success

a) Before any subject test or assignment set your own goal – what do you want to achieve?

b) Describe your goal – clearly and precisely.

....

....

c) Describe what you are going to do to achieve that goal.

....

....

d) After you get the results back, describe what your result was, sticking only to the facts.

....

....

e) Did you achieve your goal?
- Yes – that's good. You need to consider if you are setting your goals too low. Try this process again for a new academic goal
- No – this is an excellent opportunity to practice failing well – work through the following steps

f) Look at the questions you got wrong in the test or the comments the teacher wrote on your assignment and re-write each answer correctly using the textbook or your own notes to help you.

g) Take your new answers to your teacher or one of the students who got them right and check to make sure you now have the correct answers.

h) For each question you got wrong, find one more similar question in the textbook or from the teacher and do it by yourself with no help from the teacher or the text book.

i) Ask your teacher to check your answer to these new questions.

j) Once you have them right, you have learned from the experience and you can move on, but more importantly you have practiced *failing well*. Learning how to fail well and practicing failing well are the most important things you can do to guarantee academic success at school.

Self-Assessment of ATL Skills

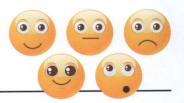

To see how best to use this page refer to pages 114 and 115.

ATL Skills	Novice *Watch*	Learner *Copy*	Practitioner *Do*				Expert *Share*
			Starting	*Practicing*	*Getting better*	*Got it!*	
Mindfulness							
Perseverance							
Impulsiveness and Anger							
Bullying							
Pressure and Stress							
Self-Motivation							
Resilience							
Failing Well							

Student Self-Assessment of ATL Skills Proficiency – AFFECTIVE SKILLS

REFLECTION SKILLS

Reflection is the process of looking back at any experience you have had, and considering what you have learned from it. From any experience, you could learn new facts, you could learn new skills, or you could learn something about how you learn.

Effective reflection is not about how good or bad you thought the experience was. It is about what new understandings you have reached from analyzing the experience in terms of both what you have learned and how you have learned it.

Reflective learners take on new understandings, relate them to what they already know, adapt them for their own purposes and translate thoughts into action. The central feature of reflection is the process of metacognition or thinking about your thinking. Through effective reflection, you are always looking for what works for you – the learning skills, techniques and strategies that help you gain new understandings – and noticing what does not work for you. The aim of reflection is to help you to improve all your learning skills in order to make learning easier and more effective for you.

Through practicing the skills in the Reflection cluster, you will learn three key metacognitive processes:

1) how to identify gaps in your knowledge by analyzing your understanding of your school subjects from the point of view of what you don't know yet, what you don't yet understand

2) how to accurately assess your own ATL skills and work on improving them to improve the effectiveness of all your learning

3) how to work out what learning strategies and techniques work best for you.

GREAT REFLECTION

The United Nations is an organization set up specifically to promote peace through dialogue, discussion and negotiation. As Sir Winston Churchill (paraphrasing George Santayana) put it: *"Those who do not learn from history are doomed to repeat it."*

Learning lessons from history is a great example of using reflection to promote the greater good. The United Nations was established on October 24, 1945, after the end of World War II, initially as a group of 51 allied nations whose goal was to make sure that another world war never occurred.

Today there are 193 member states in the UN whose objectives are to maintain international peace and security, promote human rights, encourage social and economic development, protect the environment and provide humanitarian aid in cases of famine, natural disaster and armed conflict.

For students at school, participation in the Model United Nations, or MUN, is a great way to learn about diplomacy, international relations and the United Nations. MUN is an educational simulation or academic competition in which students from all over the world work together researching real world problems and practicing critical thinking, negotiation, debate, presentation, teamwork, leadership and effective reflection. If you want to know more go to http://www.unausa.org/global-classrooms-model-un

ATL Skills Development

5d – Try new ATL skills and evaluate their effectiveness.

5f – Consider ATL skills development.

Mastery

You will know you are at the **Expert** level in the use of this ATL skill set when, anytime you are learning something new, you notice that you are consciously aware of:

i.   all the ATL skills that you need to use to learn the new material and

ii. your own proficiency with each ATL skill needed and

iii. which skills you have mastered already and the skill in which you need more practice in using to reach the proficiency you need to learn the new material effectively and efficiently.

Exercise 1 – Self-Assessment of ATL skills

a) turn to the ATL self-assessment framework at the end of the chapter you are working on at present – it looks like this:

Student Self-Assessment of ATL Skills Proficiency							
ATL Skills	**Novice** *Watch*	**Learner** *Copy*	**Practitioner** *Do*				**Expert** *Share*
			Starting	*Practicing*	*Getting better*	*Got it!*	

b) look in the first column and find the name of the ATL skill on which your teachers are currently having you work.

c) turn to the page in this book where that ATL skill is described and look at what is written at the top of the page under the heading, Mastery. This describes the performance level that you would have to reach to consider yourself an Expert in the use of that particular ATL skill.

d) using the following checklist, work out where you are right now in your development of that particular ATL skill and put a check (or a cross) and today's date in the correct box in your self-assessment.

Level 1 – The Novice *Watch*	Level 2 – The Learner *Copy*	Level 3 – The Practitioner *Do*				Level 4 – The Expert *Share*
		Starting	*Practicing*	*Getting better*	*Got it!*	
I know what the use of the skill looks like when others are using it.	I can copy someone else using the skill.	I am starting to use the skill by myself.	I am using the skill by myself in familiar situations.	I am getting better at using the skill in unfamiliar situations.	I am able to use the learning skill whenever I need to.	I use the skill without needing to think it through first.
I can break the skill down into steps.	I use the skill one step at a time.	I am still conscious of using the skill one step at a time.	I am starting to put all the steps of the skill together.	I can usually use the skill without referring to the way that I have done it in the past.	I can confidently use the skill without referring to the way I have done it before.	I am capable of teaching other students how to use the skill.
When I try to use the skill myself I make lots of mistakes and ask lots of questions.	I still make mistakes and ask for help but I am getting better at correcting my own mistakes.	I can correct my mistakes with some help.	I can correct my own mistakes.	Any mistakes I make I can quickly correct.	I can usually correct any mistakes automatically.	I correct any mistakes I make automatically.
I need lots of help to use the skill.	I can use the skill in familiar situations with some help.	I still need help to use the skill sometimes.	I don't need help to use the skill in familiar situations anymore.	I still need help to use the skill in unfamiliar situations sometimes.	I hardly ever need help to use the skill anymore.	I can use the skill in unfamiliar situations without any help from anyone else.

e) Then do a self-assessment of the next ATL skill the same way.

f) Do another self-assessment of the same ATL skills in a couple of weeks (or when the teacher asks you to) and notice your improvement.

g) At home, use the practice exercises on each page in this textbook to improve your skill proficiency.

h) When you get to the **Expert** level in any ATL skill, see if you can find a classmate whose proficiency in the use of that skill you could help to improve. Remember that no-one is ever good with every ATL skill and they might be able to help you to develop some of your own skills in return.

Always challenge yourself to learn new ATL skills. Remember the more ATL skills you have, the better you will be at learning every subject and the better your performance in all your subjects will be.

Reflection on Content

5e – Consider content
   i.   What did I learn about today?
   ii. What don't I yet understand?
   iii. What questions do I have now?

Mastery

You will know you are at the **Expert** level in the use of this ATL skill when you automatically check any new work to make sure you understand it all, you look for any parts you don't yet understand, you formulate questions to fill in the gaps in your own understanding, and you make sure you find the answers to your questions.

Reflection is most useful when it leads to new understandings. This is only possible if you become very clear about what you do understand and, more importantly, about what you don't yet understand. This is the critical part. Have you ever been struggling to understand a whole new topic and had one of those moments where one little part of the topic becomes clear to you and suddenly you make sense of the whole topic? What has happened, of course, is that you have found the key to your own understanding and that has unlocked an entire topic. The keys to understanding are what you are always seeking, and you need to be aware that they will be different for different people.

If you want to learn how to do this in a systematic way with anything that you are finding difficult, then the most important skills to learn are:

1) the skill of analyzing your own present understandings – by becoming clear about the things you do understand but, even more important, working out what the pieces are that you don't yet understand. And then...

2) the skill of asking the right question, the answer to which will fill in the gap you have identified in your own understanding.

Exercise 1 – What I don't understand yet

a) looking back over a certain piece of work you have just completed – one lesson, one topic, one concept – fill in the first line first then answer any of the following questions that are relevant to you:

1) The parts I understood well were...

....

■ But the words I still don't really understand yet are...

....

■ The ideas I don't understand yet are ....

....

■ How do I ....

....

■ What do I have to do to..

....

■ What I need to know is..

....

■ The thing I just don't get is ....

....

■ What do you mean when you say ....

....

2) See if you can write a specific question which, if you got a clear answer to it, would clear up your lack of understanding in this area.

In order to understand this (lesson, topic, concept), I need to understand ....

....

....

3) Find the resources or the explanation you need to answer your question. See if you can get an answer that makes sense to you from:

o   a teacher

o   a friend

o   an older student

o   an adult – someone who knows something about the subject

o   the textbook

o   the internet

(Do **2d – Help others to succeed** on page 51 to find someone in your class that might be able to help you)

4) Focus on the way you are processing the information, the techniques you are using to read, make useful notes, summarize key points, remember important concepts and facts. Try different ways of learning until you find a way that helps you to understand.

5) Write out an explanation, in your own words, of the part that you previously didn't understand.

6) Check your new understanding with your teacher or another student.

Creation through Imitation

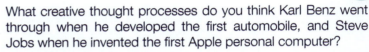

5h – Focus on the process of creating by imitating the work of others.

Mastery

You will know you are at the **Expert** level in the use of this ATL skill when you can confidently understand the creative thought processes of others and use similar processes in your own work.

What creative thought processes do you think Karl Benz went through when he developed the first automobile, and Steve Jobs when he invented the first Apple personal computer?

Most of the time people focus on the end product, not so much on the thought processes involved in its creation. Everything begins with an idea, so the first step of the process is thinking about what the initial idea was. Pushing your thinking beyond product to process enables you to tap into these insights to use in your own work to add depth and enhance it.

Exercise 1 – Investigating existing devices

In pairs, decide on something that has been created that you could investigate. It could be a new or an old invention, a piece of software or an app, a food product, an electrical device, a vehicle or anything else. All inventions or products are created to meet needs. Some of these needs are easily identified as problems to be solved, some are needs of which people are not even aware.

a) Imagine you are the person who created this thing and describe the problem they wanted to solve or the need they had identified:

....

....

....

b) Describe the solution that was eventually arrived at:

....

....

c) Creation is one part imagination and one part logical, step-by-step development. Can you imagine what the steps were that the creator of this thing had to go through to get from a) to b)? What would have been some of the problems they would have faced or obstacles they would have had to overcome? What were the solutions they came up with?

The problem/need identified		
The final solution		
Steps	**Problems/Obstacles**	**Solutions**
1		
2		
3		
4		
5		

Exercise 2 – Standing on the shoulders of giants

One way to be creative is to take an existing idea or product and think of a way to improve it, to make it solve a new problem or meet a different need. Try taking the thing you described in Exercise 1 and extending it, modifying it in some way using your own creativity.

a) What are the steps you would have to go through to get the new product created? What would be the problems or obstacles you would need to overcome? What are your possible solutions?

The product as it is right now		
The new problem/need that it might be used for		
The new features that the product would need to have		

Steps	Problems/Obstacles	Solutions
1		
2		
3		
4		
5		

Exercise 3 – Your own invention

In pairs, you are going to become inventors and use the creative thinking process used in Exercises 1 & 2 to begin with a problem and finish with a possible solution. There may be many different directions your thinking may take. That doesn't matter. There are no rights or wrongs.

a) First identify a problem or a need that is, as yet, uncatered to at your school, at home, in your community or in the world in general. Then imagine the perfect solution and work your way through all the steps you would have to take to get from one to the other:

The problem/need identified		
The final solution		

Steps	Problems/Obstacles	Solutions
1		
2		
3		
4		
5		

b) How easy or difficult did you find this process?

....

c) How would you describe your own creative, idea generation process?

....

Consider Implications

5i – Consider ethical, cultural and environmental implications.

Mastery

You will know you are at the **Expert** level in the use of this ATL skill when you can look at any issue, situation, event or action and automatically understand its ethical, cultural and environmental implications.

"Considering implications" means thinking about the consequences, conclusions or actions that may result from a particular issue, situation, event or action. "Ethical implications" means considering moral questions like right and wrong, equality and fairness. "Cultural implications" means considering possible harmony or clashes with particular cultural beliefs or values. "Environmental implications" means considering the effect on the environment.

Exercise 1 – Local politics

a) Look back at a recent decision taken by your local city council or your state or national government and analyze it in terms of all the actions that will probably ensue as a result of the decision and all possible ethical, cultural and environmental implications.

Describe the decision ...				
Describe four actions that will most likely come from the decision	ACTION 1	ACTION 2	ACTION 3	ACTION 4
Ethical implications – are these resulting actions fair to all, equal, morally right?				
Cultural implications – do they affect people from different cultures differently, is any culture disadvantaged?				
Environmental implications – do they affect the environment? If so, how?				

Exercise 2 – At school

a) Look back at a recent decision made by your school administrators or an existing school rule and analyze it in terms of all the actions that happen as a result of the decision and all possible ethical, cultural and environmental implications.

Describe the decision or rule...				
Describe four actions that students or teachers take that relate to the decision	ACTION 1	ACTION 2	ACTION 3	ACTION 4
Ethical implications – are these resulting actions fair to all, equal, morally right?				
Cultural implications – do they affect people from different cultures differently, is any culture disadvantaged?				
Environmental implications – do they affect the environment? If so, how?				

b) What are the conclusions that you draw about the particular decision on which you focused?

....

....

....

c) If you think the decision needs to be reviewed, how could you write up your findings in such a way that the decision-making body would be willing to look at and consider them?

....

....

....

....

....

Journaling

5j – Keep a journal to record reflections.

Mastery

You will know you are at the **Expert** level in the use of this ATL skill when you regularly write down useful, practical reflections that help you to improve your learning.

The most useful type of reflection is that which improves your learning and your success both at school and outside of school. To do this you need to be aware of your own processes (your thoughts, feelings and actions) at any given moment and record what works best for you. The simplest rule is to do more of what works and less of what doesn't work. If you do this in all areas of your life, you will be successful.

Exercise 1 – Keep a journal

a) You first need to decide where, and in what form, you are going to keep your journal – on paper, in a diary, on your phone, laptop or tablet. It doesn't really matter where you keep it as long as you make entries as often as possible, preferably on a daily basis, and make sure all the entries are useful to you – things that will help improve your learning and success, however you see success for yourself.

Exercise 2 – Reflection on attitudes and behaviors

a) With a partner use brainstorming to come up with all the positive attitudes and behaviors that you believe a determined and engaged student would show at school, at home and in the community

....

....

....

b) For a week, to building journaling as a habit, record every time you observe yourself showing these positive attitudes and behaviors.

Exercise 3 – Reflection on success and failure

a) It would probably be useful for you to first work your way through ATL skill *4.4a,b,c – Self-Motivation* on page 101; and *4.5a,c,d – Resilience* on page 107 to learn how to keep yourself positive and how to "fail well."

b) Once you have done that, you can work your way through the next table recording your thoughts, feelings and actions around success and failure, making sure you focus on learning from each experience.

Some of my areas of satisfaction – successes or goals achieved.	What I was thinking at the time.	How I felt at the time.	What I did at the time.	What I learned from that.
1.				
2.				
3.				
4.				
5.				
Some of my areas of dissatisfaction – failures or goals not achieved.				
1.				
2.				
3.				
4.				
5.				

Exercise 4 – Reflection on the learning process

a) It would probably be useful for you now to work your way through ATL skill exercises *3i, 5a,c,g, 6d – Learning Preferences* on page 79; *5d,f – ATL Skills Development* on page 114; and *5e – Reflection on content* on page 116 to learn how to effectively reflect on what you learn and how you learn, so that your learning improves in all areas.

b) Then, to build journaling as a habit, make sure you record one thing every day that you have done that you think of as a success and one thing that you could learn from and do differently next time.

Self-Assessment of ATL Skills

To see how best to use this page refer to pages 114 and 115.

ATL Skills	Novice *Watch*	Learner *Copy*	Practitioner *Do*				Expert *Share*
			Starting	*Practicing*	*Getting better*	*Got it!*	
Student Self-Assessment of ATL Skills Proficiency – REFLECTION SKILLS							
ATL Skills Development							
Reflection on Content							
Creation through Imitation							
Consider Implications							
Journaling							

INFORMATION LITERACY SKILLS

Information literacy means having the right skills to be able to recognize when information is needed and what information is needed, to be able to search for it, locate it, evaluate, verify and validate it, and then, finally, to be able to use that information effectively.

Since the internet became a world-wide phenomenon in 1994, the skills of information literacy have become probably the most significant skills needed in modern education, research and business. People with high-level information literacy skills are in great demand in every area of commerce and industry, and will be even more valuable in the future as internet-based services expand into every area of our lives. It is hard to imagine how anyone without these skills will be able to work in any job except manual labor in the future.

The biggest problem with the increasing reliance on the internet as our primary information source, is the unfiltered nature of that information which raises questions about accuracy, authenticity, validity and reliability. The sheer abundance of information available will not necessarily produce more informed people and a better informed society without the complementary skills needed to use that information effectively.

By practicing the skills in this cluster, you will get better at researching – you will learn how to use the right tools to help limit the results of any search down to exactly the information you need. You will learn how to verify the accuracy of any information you find, how to analyze, process and make connections, how to use information to make good decisions and how to reference that information in reports and other documents. Within this cluster are also the skills of how to process information using your preferred sensory system of thinking, as well as the skills you need to create a great memory of information you need for tests and exams.

All these skills will make a great difference in your ability to research effectively and work independently, in a self-regulated manner, working by yourself or in a team.

GREAT INFORMATION

The success of the internet is totally dependent on information storage and data transmission rates. This necessitates the construction of huge "data-farms" containing thousands of CPUs needed to process and store information.

The performance of these data farms is directly linked to their ability to dissipate the heat they generate and so some of the largest (and most environmentally friendly) of these installations are built in cold climates to enable cooling of the CPUs using cold ambient air – like the Facebook facility which is built on the edge of the Arctic Circle in Northern Sweden.

Collect, Record and Verify

z

Mastery

You will know you are at the **Expert** level in the use of this ATL skill when you can find exactly the information you want at any time and verify its accuracy.

While much research in the 21st century is done using search engines, it is also important to understand how to research using hard copy resources such as books and journals. You need to be aware of how all libraries use the Dewey Decimal Classification System to organize information – including electronic resources, documents and books – into classes and subjects.

For online resources, you need to be able to select the best words to narrow your search, understand the results you find, search for evidence and check the accuracy of the data found. The data sourced from the internet is not always credible. Keep in mind that almost anyone can publish on the internet and it is often difficult to find out who created what information and to separate opinion from facts. It is the user's responsibility to evaluate and verify any data collected.

Exercise 1 – The library – Dewey Classification

a) Either go to a library yourself or ask one of your teachers to invite your librarian to your class to explain how the Dewey Decimal Classification System works.

b) What are the ten classes into which that information is organized?

1. .... 2. ....
3. .... 4. ....
5. .... 6. ....
7. .... 8. ....
9. .... 10. ....

c) For each of the following knowledge types write in the Dewey classification code.

1. Physics topics... 2. "Gone With the Wind" ....

3. Peru... 4. Leonardo Da Vinci ....

5. Computer coding... 6. Mental health..

7. Pyramids... 8. Frisbees ....

9. Buddhism .... 10. The psychology of learning.....................

d) Ask your librarian what are the best ways to check the accuracy and credibility of the data you research.

Exercise 2 – Internet search

a) How do you currently search for anything on the internet?...

....

b) How many results do you usually get – on average? ....

....

c) How many results do you usually look at?..

....

Effective internet searching is a combination of picking the right search terms, narrowing your search, understanding the results you get and verifying the credibility of what you find.

Exercise 3 – Narrowing your search

a) Do an internet search for "Boolean Operators," "Search Limiters" and "Advanced Search Tips." Write 10 examples of each into the following table and how each one can be used:

Boolean Operators		Search Limiters		Advanced Search Tips	
Operator	How to use it	Limiter	How to use it	Tip	How to use it

b) Get together with a partner and compare results. Did they get any that you missed? Add any useful ones you get from your partner.

Exercise 4 – Verifying data

a) Working with your partner and using the search-narrowing skills you learned in the last exercise, search for the best ways to verify each aspect of internet source validity listed below. Fill in the table as you go.

What to check and verify	How to check and verify – what evidence would you need?
Author or authors	
Purpose – why was this particular piece written?	
Objectivity – is the information fact, opinion or one point of view?	
Credibility – is the information well researched?	
Currency – how up-to-date is the information?	
Links – are they current and valid?	
Conclusion – is it supported?	

b) Get together with another pair and compare results. See what you agree on.

c) Do the same again with another group of four.

d) Write up what you agree are the best ways to verify data.

e) Write them up as a series of tips and post them on the wall of your classroom. Ask for comments.

Exercise 5 – Your own work

a) The next time you are researching on the internet make sure you practice the best ways to limit your search and verify what you find.

Access and Connect

6b – Access information to be informed and inform others.
6c – Make connections between various sources of information.

Mastery

You will know you are at the **Expert** level in the use of this ATL skill set when you can easily see patterns in information through connections and comparisons.

One purpose of accessing information is to make connections with other information – to be more informed and to inform others. Extending your understanding of any topic requires you to collect more information about it to broaden your overview of it.

Exercise 1 – International news

a) Work in pairs.

b) Pick one current international news topic and find six different places which have reported on it.

c) Analyze each different report of the same event and describe how they are all connected and how they are different.

News event name and date	How are these reports connected – what do they agree on?	How is each one different?
Source 1		
Source 2		
Source 3		
Source 4		
Source 5		
Source 6		

Exercise 2 – Connections between topics

a) Work in pairs with each person researching a different topic in which they are interested.

b) Research each topic and write in the boxes any information that answers the questions Who, What, Where, When, Why & How.

c) When you have both finished your research, work together and draw lines in the box inbetween to make any connections between the information you have found, write along the line what the connection is. Any connection at all is OK – be creative.

	Topic 1	Connections	Topic 2
Who			
What			
Where			
When			
Why			
How			

Memory Techniques

Mastery

You will know you are at the **Expert** level in the use of this ATL skill when you automatically use memory techniques and cycles of review whenever necessary to help you remember information well.

Remembering your schoolwork requires the application of several ATL skills. First you need to realize that the key to remembering is understanding, and the first step in developing understanding is making sure you are creating summary notes in your own words. Once you understand things well, you need to get the information into long-term memory through the application of regular review – going over the key points again and explaining them to yourself in your own words. Lastly, for any lists of facts you need to remember by rote, you can apply good memory techniques.

Exercise 1 – Building review schedules for study

a) It would be most useful for you to first work on the best, most effective method for you to make your summary notes or study notes (work through *1.2i – Take effective notes in class* and *1.2j – Make effective notes for studying* on page 33).

b) Second, you need to get yourself to regularly create summaries of key points in every subject – as preparation for assessments or as part of your own schedule of review.

c) As soon as you have made a good summary of a topic you need to make sure you understand it well by explaining it to yourself – read through your summary and, out loud, turn your summary back into sentences – explain it to yourself in your own words.

d) For any parts you don't yet understand, go back to the text book or the original notes and pull out a few more words to add to your summary. Then explain that part to yourself again.

e) Within 24 hours of making the summary, look at it again and explain it to yourself again in your own words.

f) One week after you made the summary the first time, look at it again and explain it to yourself again in your own words.

g) One month after you made the summary the first time, look at it again and explain it to yourself again in your own words.

By this stage you will definitely have the information in long-term memory.

h) Test your understanding by doing an old exam question on the topic you have studied. Write out a good answer to the question without referring back to your notes. Check your answer with your notes.

Exercise 2 – Memory techniques

There are many different memory techniques you can use to help you. Here are three:

a) Number Pegging

i. Create a series of images in your mind to represent the numbers from 1-10 – e.g.

one	two	three	four	five	six	seven	eight	nine	ten
drum	shoe	tree	door	hive	sticks	heaven	gate	sign	hen

Repeat that over to yourself a couple of times until you have them fixed.

Now use those "pegs" to help you remember important dates in history.

The method involves simply picturing the particular historical event and including in that picture a representation of the date as the number pegs from the last example.

ii.   e.g. Invention of the printing press – 1439

1439 using our system is Drum – Door – Tree – Sign

You probably don't need to create a picture for the first number 1 because any date you are trying to remember for school will usually start with 1 so all you need to remember is 439 – Door – Tree – Sign, but you need to get those numbers in the correct order. The trick with this technique is to make the picture you use as specific and imaginative as possible. e.g.

Imagine that you are in an old town in Europe in the middle ages, all dirty and smoky, and you are outside a big factory building and you can hear the noise of a machine clanking and crashing inside the building. You drag open a huge wooden door and inside the building you see that all the noise is coming from an enormous printing press, crashing and banging while it is shooting out hundreds of books onto the floor. It looks like it is out of control and just about to explode and you look around for who is in charge of the machine and see that the foreman is sleeping under a huge oak tree in the middle of the factory floor. A sign next to the tree reads "DANGER – FLYING BOOKS!" while the foreman sleeps on and the printing press is out of control and about to explode. Make sure you can picture the door, the tree and the sign in that order and all linked to the printing press.

iii. Try making up your own silly picture stories for:
The invention of the telescope. *1608: Sticks – Hen – Gate*
The invention of the sewing machine. *1790: Heaven – Sign – Hen*
The invention of the lawnmower. *1830: Gate – Tree – Hen*

b) Method of Loci

This is another type of memory system which allows you to use locations that are very familiar to you as mental locations for information you want to remember.

i.   What you need to do first is create a list of places you know well. Imagine you are at home, taking a walk through your house. Can you make a list of 10 things that you would see in the order you would see them (e.g. the back door, the kitchen table, the bench, the stovetop, the kitchen sink, the dishwasher) Try doing that now. Write them under "Places" in the table below.

ii. Having done that, what you need to do is create a list of ten grocery items that you might buy in the supermarket (e.g. eggs, chocolate, sausages, butter, fish, soda, etc.) and write them under "Items" in the table, one for each location – fill in your own information into the table:

For example:	
Places	Items
Back door	Eggs
Table	Chocolate
Bench	Sausages
Stove	Butter
Sink	Fish
Dishwasher	Soda

Places	Items	Places	Items

iii. Then all you have to do is imagine walking through your house and put one grocery item in each place (in your imagination), but put them there in as 'over-the-top' an image as possible e.g.

I opened up the back door and crashed it into a pile of eggs. The eggs all broke and there was a sticky, gooey mess oozing all over the back step. So, I carefully stepped over that and went into the kitchen. The first thing I saw was the kitchen table which was made of chocolate so I broke a piece off and ate it and then looked at the bench which I noticed was made of hundreds of sausages all stacked up together. Then I saw the stove with a pot full of melted butter and the butter was spilling out of the pot and burning on the hot element. So, I turned around to the sink to get some water but the sink was full of fish swimming. So, I opened the dishwasher and gallons of soda poured out all over the floor ...

iv. Imagine your list of grocery items in order, in your house, imagine them as vividly as possible. Then cover up your table and test yourself, close your eyes and take a walk through your house in your mind and see if all the items are there.

v.   Open your eyes and test yourself, can you remember all the items now in order? How about in backwards order?

c) Using a Picture Story for Physics

i. A physics student made up the following way to remember all the forms and types of energy there are on earth. Try it yourself and see if it works for you:

Imagine the sun plugged into an electrical socket in the sky getting hotter and hotter and hotter until it gets so hot it blasts off and races across the sky screaming "GET OUT OF MY WAY" to all the clouds. It races away until it comes to a screeching stop at the edge of the sky where there is a huge drop. So, it ties a bungee cord onto its feet and bungees over the edge. It bounces up and down many times but it is so hot that it burns through the bungee cord and drops down and down until it falls into a vat of acid and causes a big bubbling, hissing, smelly, chemical reaction and eventually it all explodes in a giant nuclear explosion.

ii. What you will now find is that:

1) the Active Energies are: *... the sun (**Solar**) plugged into an electrical socket (**Electrical**) in the sky getting hotter and hotter and hotter (**Heat**) until it gets so hot it blasts off and races across the sky (**Kinetic**) screaming "GET OUT OF MY WAY" (**Sound**) to all the clouds. It races away until it comes to a screeching stop at the edge of the sky where there is a huge drop ...*

2) the Potential Energies are: *... so it ties a bungee cord onto its feet and jumps (**Gravitational**) over the edge, it bounces up and down (**Elastic**) many times but it is so hot that it burns through the bungee cord and drops down and down until ...*

3) the Chemical Energies are: *... it falls into a vat of acid and causes a big bubbling, hissing, smelly, chemical reaction (**Chemical**) and eventually it all explodes in a giant nuclear explosion (**Nuclear**).*

d) The Memory Castle – build your own memory castle

This is a visual thinking technique that can help you to remember information from each of your subjects accurately, and easily.

Go to ***Visual Thinking – Exercise 2*** on page 203 to see how to create your own Memory Castle.

e) Once you have decided what you need to memorize – search for the right technique online. Someone will have created a way for you to memorize whatever you need to. You just have to find it.

Formats and Platforms

6f – Present information in a variety of formats and platforms.
1.2l – Find information for disciplinary and interdisciplinary inquiries, using a variety of media.

Information is found in two main forms, print and non-print. Printed materials can be in the form of books, articles, reports, journals, etc. Non-print materials can be in the form of images, video, recorded sound, podcasts, audio-visual, multimedia, etc.

Platforms include the technology, software applications and apps through which information can be presented to audiences. There is a growing choice of technology platforms upon which you can build innovative and engaging presentations of information.

The word media can be used to mean either or both of these – the form in which your message is represented to an audience and the platform you use to get your message across.

Mastery

You will know you are at the **Expert** level in the use of this ATL skill set when you can confidently identify the most appropriate and effective formats and platforms with which to present your information.

Exercise 1 – Multimedia school work

a) Work with a partner.
b) Each of you take one simple fact from any subject and see how many ways you can find that fact represented – see who can find the most.
c) Take one whole topic and do the same.
d) Indicate which form of the information made it easiest to understand for you.

	I found this in...						The one that worked best for me was
Person 1 – my fact is ...							
Person 2 – my fact is ...							
Person 1 – my topic is ...							
Person 2 – my topic is ...							

Exercise 2 – Changing media

a) First take one presentation you have already made and transpose it onto a different presentation platform – swap between Prezi, Powerpoint, Google Slides, Keynote, etc.

b) Then take the same presentation and reproduce it as printed media – a book, series of pictures, storyboard, etc.

c) Evaluate each information delivery media in terms of positives, negatives and what you thought the impact on the audience would be.

d) Which is your preferred delivery media?

	Advantages	Disadvantages	Impact on the audience	My preferred media for delivery of information is ...
My original presentation was made using ...				
The presentation platform I changed it to was ...				
The printed media format I changed it to was ...				

Exercise 3 – Multimedia

a) To practice using multimedia in presentations, do the exercises in *1.1e – Use a variety of media to communicate with a range of audiences* on page 10; and *1.1c – Use a variety of speaking techniques to communicate with a variety of audiences* on page 5.

Sources and Tools

6i – Evaluate and select information sources and digital tools based on their appropriateness to specific tasks.

Mastery

You will know you are at the **Expert** level in the use of this ATL skill when you can confidently select the most appropriate sources of information and digital technologies to process that information for each of your academic tasks.

You can tap into a variety of sources to access the information you need. These include websites, blogs, newspapers, books, magazines and so on. The key is for you to evaluate which are the most appropriate ones for your needs and what to look for within each one.

There is also a variety of digital tools you can use to generate, process and store information to help with your learning, including many different software apps, information sharing and communication platforms as well as social media. You need to become good at selecting the best tools and sources for the tasks you have to complete.

HOME	PORTFOLIO	BLOG	CONTACTS

Exercise 1 – Research and verify

a) It would be useful for you to first do the exercises in *6a – Collect, record and verify data* on page 126 to learn about how to find the information you need and how to verify its accuracy and credibility.

Exercise 2 – Information tasks and needs

a) Think about the assignments and projects you have going at present – what information do you need for each one? Do the following analysis for two pieces of academic work you have going at the moment:

Give each one a title	1.	2.
What is the question you are trying to answer?		
What information will you need to find to answer the question?		

Think of two different places (sources) where you could find that information			
What is one advantage and one disadvantage of each source			
What do you need to do with the information? Analyze, summarize, copy?			
Think of two different digital tools (apps or programs) you could use to do this.			
What is one advantage and one disadvantage of each digital tool?			
Which combination of source and digital tool is best for each assignment?			

Analyze and Interpret

6k – Use critical literacy skills to analyze and interpret media communications.
7b – Demonstrate awareness of media interpretations of events and ideas (including digital social media).
7e – Seek a range of perspectives from multiple and varied sources.

Mastery

You will know you are at the **Expert** level in the use of this ATL skill set when you automatically seek out the most appropriate media for the information you need based on your own analysis of its accuracy, validity, interpretation and possible bias.

When you are processing information gathered from different media, you are always using a collection of different ATL skills, (hopefully) working together as a team. The aim is to develop the skills necessary to analyze the gathered information and identify the strengths and weaknesses of the argument presented, check the validity of the data presented, recognize any unfounded assumptions or bias and find any trends, patterns or valid predictions.

It would be an advantage to first get familiar with *8c,e,g,h – Evaluating Assumptions* on page 163; and *8b,f – Formulating Arguments* on page 161; as well as *8r – Identify trends and forecast possibilities* on page 165.

Exercise 1 – Investigating bias

a) Find one big recent international news story and look at how it is presented in four different news media. Use the website of your own country's biggest newspaper as one source and choose three other sources from the following – Al Jazeera, BBC, Fox, RT.

b) Research each media source and find out who they represent – by whom they are owned and who is their target audience.

c) Then analyze the story using the following table.

Media sources chosen:	1.	2.	3.	4.
By whom are they each owned?				
Who is each one's target audience?				
What is the news story about?				
What was each one's headline?				
What was each one's main story?				

What was the evidence presented?			
If there was a conclusion drawn or prediction made, what was it?			
Can you identify any bias or assumptions in the reporting?			
Did the media look equally at both sides of the event or issue?			
How valid do you think the argument presented was?			
Which media do you think presented the most well-balanced, well-researched report?			

Exercise 2 – Other media representations

a) Find comments on the same news story on five different social media and photo-sharing platforms.

b) What type and form of information does each media platform seek to give to the reader?

c) On what aspect of the news story has each media platform been focused?

d) If this was the only information to which you had access on this news story, what conclusion might you draw about the event?

Platform chosen: social media or photo-sharing	Type and form of information provided?	On what did the comments or photos focus?	What conclusion might you draw?
1.			
2.			
3.			
4.			
5.			

IP Referencing

Mastery

You will know you are at the **Expert** level in the use of this ATL skill set when you automatically recognize others' intellectual property rights, respect and acknowledge them and construct accurate referencing in your bibliography.

Intellectual property (IP) rights describe protection (copyright, patents, trademarks, etc.) given to original works. These can be writings, artistic works, musical compositions, inventions, designs, images, symbols, names, etc., created by any person. As soon as you create something, it is automatically protected by copyright which means no-one else can copy it and use it without your permission, and, if they do, you may take action against them. When you publish any information in print or on the internet, you have the right to make it freely available to anyone or make it subject to IP law. When you want to copy any information or images from books, journals, magazines or the internet, you need to check first if it is covered by copyright or not. If you are not copying – you are using someone else's ideas but interpreting them in your own way – copyright is not involved. But when you do use any ideas or images that are not your own, it is very important to reference where you got them and who created them. Referring to another author or piece of work within your own work is called citation. All citations are then collected and referenced fully in the bibliography. Copying or using others IP without acknowledging it is called plagiarism.

Exercise 1 – Intellectual property

a) When you download music or videos are you automatically breaking copyright law? .... ☐ YES ☐ NO

b) If you were streaming the same material, would you automatically be breaking copyright law? .... ☐ YES ☐ NO

c) How and why are the two systems (downloading and streaming) different?

....

....

....

....

d) In what circumstances can you download or stream material without breaking copyright law?

....

....

....

e) If you cut and paste words or images directly from a website are you automatically breaking copyright law? ☐ YES ☐ NO

f) What can you do with information you take from any website to make sure you are not breaking copyright law?

....

....

....

Exercise 2 – Referencing

a) Get hold of a copy of the rules for your school's preferred referencing system.

b) Find one example of each of the information types listed below and write the information you find and the full reference in the table below using the rules from (a).

Information type and source	What is the information?	Create a full reference
One fact copied directly from one non-fiction book on any topic		
One quote taken from any fiction book		
One conclusion from one paper found in any scientific journal		
One headline from any newspaper		
One direct quote from any TV news program		
One direct quote from any website		
One direct quote from any blog		
One opinion from any social media platform		
Any non-copyrighted video clip		
Any non-copyrighted song		

Identify Sources

Mastery

You will know you are at the **Expert** level in the use of this ATL skill when you can automatically distinguish between primary and secondary resources.

Primary sources are firsthand (or first to record) accounts of a situation, event or issue. They are the author's writing about his or her own experience in the form of a diary, a speech, a letter, a journal, an interview, etc.

Secondary sources are interpretations of primary source information. Secondary source materials analyze, compare and contrast primary source information and draw conclusions or predictions as a result. These are found in the form of published papers in journals, articles in magazines, books, blogs, documentaries, films, etc. Textbooks are always secondary sources of information. See *6l,m – IP Referencing* on page 139 for how to reference correctly.

Exercise 1 – Textbooks

a) Take any subject textbook

b) Skim through the text in any chapter until you find a citation – where the author has referred to another person's work, discovery or invention – and given the reference.

- Name of textbook, author (full reference) ....
  ....

- Citation (full reference) ....
  ....

- What is the claim made for the cited author? ....
  ....
  ....

c) Now you need to research and find the piece of work referenced to in the citation, skim through it and answer these questions:

- Is the citation a primary or secondary source for the claim in the textbook? ....
  ....

- If it is a secondary source, you need to find whom they cite and follow that reference until you get to the primary source of the information ....
  ....

- The primary source of the information is (full reference) ....
  ....
  ....

- Did the textbook reference this work correctly? ....
  ....
  ....

d) Do the same exercise over again but with a different textbook.

Exercise 2 – Your own work

a) Take one recent piece of your own work, in any subject – one that had two or more referenced claims.

b) For each reference, determine if it is a primary or secondary source.

c) If it is a secondary source, use your research skills to track back until you find the primary source of the evidence.

d) What is the evidence that proves your source is a primary source?

Reference	Claim	Primary or Secondary	If Secondary, what is the Primary reference?	What is the evidence that proves the primary source
Ref 1:				
Ref 2:				

Self-Assessment of ATL Skills

To see how best to use this page refer to pages 114 and 115.

Student Self-Assessment of ATL Skills Proficiency – INFORMATION LITERACY SKILLS							
ATL Skills	**Novice** *Watch*	**Learner** *Copy*	**Practitioner** *Do*				**Expert** *Share*
			Starting	*Practicing*	*Getting better*	*Got it!*	
Collect, Record and Verify							
Access and Connect							
Memory Techniques							
Formats and Platforms							
Sources and Tools							
Analyze and Interpret							
IP Referencing							
Identify Sources							

Notes

MEDIA LITERACY SKILLS

The word media can mean both the means by which you receive messages – written word, spoken word, music, visual images, video, animation, etc. – and the platform used to get the message to you – books, newspapers, blogs, magazines, messaging, social media, TV, websites, etc.

Media representations of information are powerful influences in all people's lives today and shape the way we view the world. To be engaged and critical media consumers, students need to develop the skills and habits of media literacy.

Media literacy is a collection of essential skills for 21st Century education which helps students learn how to access, analyze, evaluate, participate with and create messages in a variety of forms from print to video to the internet. Media literacy skills will help you gain an understanding of the role and influence of the media in modern society, and become a critical and literate consumer and producer of all media forms. This will enable you to learn to control the interpretation of all the messages you see and hear rather than letting the interpretation control you. In this cluster you will learn the skills of effective media consumption including how to access a wide range of media; to critically analyze both the messages and the media as to source, reliability, interpretation, assumptions and bias; and how to evaluate media messages as to authenticity and reliability.

To become an effective media producer you will also need to gain an awareness of media impact and learn the skills of appropriate selection of media, composition of message, creativity of design and production.

GREAT MEDIA

The greatest media-based mechanism for people-to-people communication ever devised is social media. Although most people today take it completely for granted, it is instructive to realize that social media as an idea has only been around for about 15 years and that the biggest player in the field, Facebook, was created in 2004. Since then, Facebook has grown into a platform which potentially allows more than 1,300,000,000 people to communicate with each other. No communication device or media has ever reached that many people before in the whole history of humanity.

Social media is influenced by technological development and, due to the abrupt rise in mobile computing (especially photo and video sharing), the most successful new social media platforms like Snapchat, Instagram, Foursquare and Facebook hinge on the capabilities of smartphones.

Social media has changed the world of communication, hopefully for the better.

Ethical Research

7a – Locate, organize, analyze, evaluate, synthesize and ethically use information from a variety of sources and media (including digital social media and online networks).

Mastery

You will know you are at the **Expert** level in the use of this ATL skill set when you can independently and ethically use the elements of media literacy to conduct an investigation of a topic by gathering information from a variety of sources, including digital media sources.

This ATL skill set involves the amalgamation of many other ATL skills in the completion of a research task. To complete this ATL skill set, you first have to have a research project to complete. Preferably a significant project like your Personal or Community Project.

Then you need to apply and practice all of the following ATL skills – how to:

a) Locate the information you need:

1.2l – find information using a variety of media (page 133)

6a – shrink a search down to the information you really want (page 126)

6i – select the best sources and digital tools for the task (page 135)

b) Organize, analyze and evaluate the information

6h,g – process the data and make informed decisions (page 165)

6k, 8c – identify bias, assumptions and interpretations (pages 137 & 163)

8e,g,h – analyze the information you collect for the validity of the argument (page 163)

8r – identify trends and forecast possibilities (page 165)

c) Synthesize your own point of view

8b,f – formulate a valid argument (page 161)

d) And when you write this project up you are going to need to know how to:

6m – create citations, references and a bibliography (page 139)

e) When you are up to Part (c) you will need to focus on the ethical use of information. To do this, you will first need to understand and practice:

6l – intellectual property rights (page 139)

1.1h, 2a – responsible use of digital social media (page 16)

You will also need to complete the following exercises.

Exercise 1 – Ethical use

Ethical use of information means not knowingly using that information to cause any harm. For most people, harm to any persons or to the environment is considered unethical use. But that definition can also be broadened to include harm to business or industry, to animals, plants, even insects. Ethical use of information will be defined by your school, probably in a school policy document.

a) Find your school policy on the ethical use of information.

b) Compare that document with the list of top 10 rules for safe and responsible social media use that you generated in 1.1h on page 16.

c) Can you add any more ideas to the school policy? ....

....

....

Exercise 2 – Media ethics

Think of all the ways information is presented to you and consider the impact on people and on the environment of the form of each one, (e.g. food advertising is information given to you, usually printed on the packaging around food, which then has to be disposed of later, creating a waste disposal effect on the environment and an effect on people of wasting time, effort and land.)

Consider all the ways in which information can be delivered to you and the ethical implications of each one. Put all the media into a priority list based on their ethics of information delivery.

How does information come to you?	What is the impact on the environment of the delivery method used?	What is the impact on people of the delivery method used?	Rate each media on ethics of delivery from 1-10. 1 = lowest, most harm; 10 = highest, least harm.
News-paper			
Books			
Magazines			
Food Packaging			
Junk Mail			
Bill-boards			
Emails			
On-line Streaming			
Radio			
TV			

Media Choices

Mastery

You will know you are at the **Expert** level in the use of this ATL skill when you actively and accurately choose the correct media for the purpose you have in mind.

Whenever you access information of any sort, you are doing it for a reason. Becoming clear about your purpose and aware of the different perspectives available through different media will help you choose the most appropriate viewing experience.

In order to understand some of the different perspectives available on any one story, it would be useful for you to first work through **6k – Use critical literacy skills to analyze and interpret media communications**; **7b – Demonstrate awareness of media interpretations of events and ideas** and **7e – Seek a range of perspectives from multiple and varied sources** on page 137.

Exercise 1 – What do you choose?

Work your way through the table below:

a)   For each task, think of what your real goal or purpose is – why do you want to do each one?

b)   Choose one website, app or media platform for each task.

c)   Justify your choice – think of one advantage, one disadvantage and two other possible options for each.

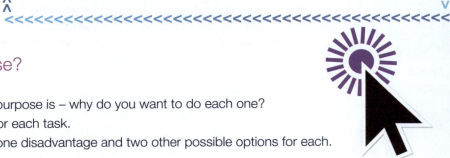

Viewing Task – if I want to find ...	My goal or purpose is ...	My best choice for this task is ...	Advantages	Disadvantages	Two other possible options
Movies					
Games					
Music					
International News					
Chat					

Viewing Task – if I want to find ...	My goal or purpose is ...	My best choice for this task is ...	Advantages	Disadvantages	Two other possible options
What people in my class are doing					
What other people think on an issue					
Information on: (list your top six school subjects)					
1.					
2.					
3.					
4.					
5.					
6.					
Any other tasks for which you use the internet:					
1.					
2.					
3.					

d)   Make sure you are choosing the best means to enable you to complete your task and achieve your goal in each case.

Media Impact

Mastery

You will know you are at the **Expert** level in the use of this ATL skill when you are constantly aware of the impact generated by certain media representations and you are able to look past the impact to find the facts.

The word media can mean both the means by which you get your message across to an audience – talking, visual images, video clips, animations, PowerPoint, etc. – and the platform you use to get your message across – a newspaper, magazine, TV, telephone, the internet, etc.

Impact on the individual comes about through emotional engagement – the greater the emotional response to the media representation, the greater the personal impact. Impact on whole populations comes about through reach – the greater the number exposed to the information, the greater the impact. Major societal change can be brought about by both the medium and the message when high emotional engagement is combined with massive reach.

Exercise 1 – Impact of different media platforms

Work in pairs, filling in the table below:

a) Column 1 – Research each of the media platforms listed below and find their reach – how many people look at them, use them, every day?

b) Column 2 – Discuss with your partner and rank each medium from one to nine as to the emotional engagement you feel with each one (9 – maximum emotional connection, 1 – minimum emotional connection)

c) Column 3-6 – Describe in the following table what you think the main impact has been of each of these media in the following areas:
   i.   communication between people
   ii.   education
   iii. privacy
   iv.   family life

	Reach	Emotional engagement	Communication between people	Education	Privacy	Family Life
Printed books						
Telephone						
Radio						
Newspapers						
Magazines						

Television						
Cell phones						
Internet						

Exercise 2 – Impact of different presentation media

Work in pairs, filling in the table below:

a) Column 1 – Research each of the media platforms listed below and find their reach – how many people look at them, use them, every day?

b) Column 2 – Discuss with your partner and rank each medium from one to nine as to the emotional engagement you feel with each one (9 – maximum emotional connection, 1 – minimum emotional connection)

c) Column 3-6 – Describe in the following table what you think the main impact has been of each of these media in the following areas:
   i.   communication between people
   ii. education
   iii. privacy
   iv. family life

	Reach	Emotional engagement	Communication between people	Education	Privacy	Family Life
Email						
Texting						
Picture texting						
Live video calling						
Instant messaging						
Streaming video						
Streaming music						
Podcasts						
Blogs						

Media Formats

7f – Communicate information and ideas effectively to multiple audiences
    using a variety of media and formats.
1.2l – Find information for disciplinary and interdisciplinary inquiries,
    using a variety of media.
7g – Compare, contrast and draw connections among (multimedia) resources.

Mastery

You will know you are at the **Expert** level in the use of this ATL skill set when you can effortlessly represent your message through many media and "translate" your message accurately between them.

How many ways are there to find information or get a message across to someone? Does the form of the message alter its meaning at all?

If you are working on this ATL skill as part of creating a presentation then it would be a good idea to do these first:

1.1e – Use a variety of media to communicate with a range of audiences on page 10.

1.1c – Use a variety of speaking techniques to communicate with a variety of audiences on page 5.

1.1j – Share ideas with multiple audiences using a variety of digital environments and media on page 18.

Then try the following exercises:

Exercise 1 – How many ways can you find information?

Work in pairs – one person researching, one person writing – swap often.

a)   Find one idea or one fact in any subject, preferably something you are not quite understanding properly yet

b)   See if you can find a representation of that fact, or a link to that fact, in all the forms suggested

c)   Analyze each representation and see if the message is the same or if a different aspect is being focused on

d)   Decide which form helped you understand the fact best

e)   Do the same for a second fact.

Can you find that fact...	Fact 1...		Fact 2...	
	Reference – where did you find it?	What is the focus of the message?	Reference – where did you find it?	What is the focus of the message?
In a paper book?				
In an e-book?				
On a website?				
In a blog?				

As a video?			
As a podcast?			
As an interactive lesson?			
In a game?			
In an on-line newspaper?			
In a movie?			

Exercise 2 – Find school work

a)   Pick any topic from any subject.

b)   Research and find four different websites based on school subjects, that have explanations of the topic.

c)   Analyze them all using this table and pick your best.

My topic is...

Does it have...	Website 1:	Website 2:	Website 3:	Website 4:
Video?				
Soundtrack or podcast?				
Written explanations?				
Animation?				

Games to play?				
Links to social media?				
Links to other students?				
Which works best for you?				

d) Do the same exercise for one topic from each of your subjects.

Exercise 3 – What is the best delivery media?

The way in which you use media in a presentation will depend on both the message to be delivered and the nature of the audience.

Work in pairs:

a) For each purpose of information delivery on the left side of this table, choose one audience group from the middle column and draw a line to connect them.

b) Discuss different delivery media, and continue the line to connect to the one you think in the third column would do the job best.

c) Try changing the audience for each message and see if that changes your preferred delivery media.

Message – purpose	Audience	Media
Informing	Pre-schoolers	Powerpoint type presentation
		Debate
Entertaining	Primary school students	Live question and answer
Teaching/learning	High school students	Written question and answer
		Social media
Advertising	University students	Video
		Music
Coaching	Fathers	Lecture
		Images
Selling	Mothers	Manipulatives – things you can hold in your hand
Social connection	Boys	Online games
Art	Girls	Physical games
		Skype
Politics	Elderly people	Independent research

Exercise 4 – Multimedia resources

Multimedia traditionally means a combination of video, still images, audio, and text working interactively to create a unique experience for the audience, but can also include information available as smell, taste, skin sensations like hot or cold, physical movement and electrical stimulation. With the introduction of holographics and virtual reality, multimedia presentations can become fully immersive for the audience and blur the line between the real and the simulated world.

a) Research multimedia – find five different multimedia platforms or systems of presentation (e.g. holograms, virtual reality) and describe their characteristics.

b) For each one, describe the type of presentation, audience or task for which it is best suited and describe its advantages and disadvantages.

Multimedia systems or platforms – describe the characteristics of each:	Best used for:	Advantages:	Disadvantages:
1.			
2.			
3.			
4.			
5.			

Self-Assessment of ATL Skills

To see how best to use this page refer to pages 114 and 115.

ATL Skills	Novice *Watch*	Learner *Copy*	Practitioner *Do*				Expert *Share*
			Starting	*Practicing*	*Getting better*	*Got it!*	
Ethical Research							
Media Choices							
Media Impact							
Media Formats							

Student Self-Assessment of ATL Skills Proficiency – MEDIA LITERACY SKILLS

CRITICAL THINKING SKILLS

Critical thinking does not mean being critical of everything and always looking for ways to criticize ideas and people. A critical thinker can still be very positive but will always want to know what the evidence is for any idea, belief or position taken by anyone else, and will want to weigh that evidence, looking at the arguments both for and against, in order to get to the truth. Critical thinkers are active inquirers and active learners who make up their own minds as to what they believe to be true, rather than being simply passive recipients of information.

To be a good critical thinker you need to be practiced in the skills of logical and analytical thinking:

- Observing and gathering data objectively
- Thinking rationally about any issue or idea from an "outsider's" point of view
- Analyzing any issue or idea to find the fundamental reasoning underlying it
- Identifying the arguments in favor of and against any particular issue or idea
- Evaluating the validity of all the arguments looking for assumptions, bias or contradictions
- Weighing all the evidence
- Drawing an evidence-based conclusion
- Providing the structured reasoning and support for any conclusion or position taken

Critical thinking is one half of the thinking required to be a good problem solver. The other half is the creative thinking required to come up with new solutions to existing problems.

Without critical thinking, creative thinking will not be practical and will not produce solutions that will work in the real world. Without creative thinking, critical thinking can result in "paralysis by analysis" where no new solutions are created and problems perpetuate.

By practicing the skills in this cluster you will become a better critical thinker and will lay the foundation for becoming a better problem solver.

GREAT CRITICAL THINKERS THAT CHANGED THE WORLD

- ➡ Albert Einstein – judgment based on facts not assumptions – theory of relativity
- ➡ Charles Darwin – evidence-based theory of natural selection – evolution
- ➡ Galileo Galilei – evidence-based argument that the Earth revolves around the sun
- ➡ Martin Luther King – "I have a dream" – great persuasive argument
- ➡ Simone de Beauvoir – equality for women – evidence-based, rational, persuasive argument
- ➡ Edwin Hubble – gathered irrefutable evidence of the expanding universe
- ➡ Marie Curie – asked the right questions, gathered conclusive experimental evidence
- ➡ Sir Isaac Newton – discovered gravity through rigorous testing
- ➡ Stanislav Petrov – trusted the facts at hand, halted mistaken nuclear counter strike by the USSR
- ➡ W. E. B. Du Bois – inspired civil rights in USA by refusing the argument of exchanging equality for legal rights.

Einstein

Observing

8a – Practice observing carefully in order to recognize problems.

Mastery

You will know you are at the **Expert** level in the use of this ATL skill when you can easily and automatically separate observations from inferences and use your observations alone to recognize any problems.

Evidence is obtained from observation using our five senses – directly, or with the assistance of tools that extend the quality or strength of our senses. For example, using a magnifying glass to make things bigger is a qualitative extension – it improves the quality of what we are observing. Using a scale to weigh an object is a quantitative extension – it gives us more information as to quantity.

An inference is a conclusion, explanation, or judgment formed from evidence. There are two types of inferences: inductive inferences involve forming a rule from the evidence available; deductive inferences involve categorizing or interpreting evidence based on a pre-existing rule and therefore involves background knowledge. Both play an important role in research.

Difference between observation and inference.

Hold up a pencil – what are your observations – long, thin, maybe yellow on the outside, brown on the inside, with a black center, pointy at one end blunt at the other? What are your inferences – made of wood, graphite, paint, called a pencil, used for drawing?

Exercise 1 – Possible observations

a) What are some observations of things that you can make by looking only?

Color, shape, size, ...

....

b) What are some observations you could make if you could only touch?

Sharp, rough, smooth, ...

....

c) How could you describe different smells? Find some words which describe different smells.

Aromatic, musty, sharp, ...

....

d) How could you describe different tastes? Find some words which describe different tastes.

Sweet, sour, ...

....

e) How could you describe different sounds? Find some words which describe different sounds.

Ringing, booming, banging, ...

....

Exercise 2 – Blind observations

a) Work in pairs. Each person needs to find one object they could use for this exercise but not show it to the other person. It should be something that is OK to touch, not sharp or dirty or yucky, and it would be best to be something slightly unusual, maybe an acorn or a dry leaf, or an unusual pen or electronic gizmo.

b) Each of you put your object in a box or under a cloth so the other person can't see what it is.

c) Each person feels the object they haven't seen and records their observations – describing the size, shape, surface features, texture, density, etc. Remember that the statements "this is made of …" and "this is ..." are not observations, but inferences.

d) Each person draws a picture of the object that is still hidden from them.

e) Each person now makes as many inferences as they can about the object – what color it might be, where it could be found, what its purpose might be used for, etc.

f) Now take the objects out and examine and note down what characteristics you can now see that were not possible to observe by touch.

g) See how accurate your inferences were.

h) What have you learned about observations and inferences?

Exercise 3 – Cartoons

a) Work in pairs. Each person needs to find a cartoon in a newspaper, the meaning of which they understand, and cut it out. Then cut off or whiteout the commentary – the words – so they are only left with the picture.

b) Swap cartoons. Paste your partner's cartoon on your page and write down what you observe and what you think is going on in the cartoon – what are your inferences?

Paste the cartoon in here

Observations – what can you see?	Inferences – what do you think is happening in the cartoon, what do you think the cartoon means – what is it about?

What is the caption? What does the cartoon really mean?

c) Now have a look at the caption and discuss what the cartoon is about.

d) How accurate were your inferences? ....

....

e) Is there anything that you now observe in the cartoon that you missed before which gives you the information you needed to make sense of it?

f) What have you now learned about observations and inferences?

Exercise 4 – Active observation

a) Work in pairs.

b) Think of one particular student crowd movement situation at school – lunchtime, break-time, between classes, after school – and consider two perspectives:
   i.   what do the students want to achieve?
   ii. what does the school want to achieve?
   Describe the objectives of each group – write them down.

c) Working as a team, position yourselves in two different places where you can both observe crowd movement well at the time you have described in (b) and observe and

record everything you see that is pertinent to the objectives stated in (b i. & ii) over a set time period.

Record how many people you see, what they are doing, how they are moving, any disruptions to the movement, etc.

d) Draw inferences from your observations and identify any problems in achieving either of the objectives from (b).

e) Compare notes – did you each identify the same problems?

f) What do you notice about observations and inferences, and the ability to use those to identify problems?

Describe the crowd movement situation and the critical time		What are the student's objectives?	What are the school's objectives?
Observations	**Inferences**	Does this help achieve the students' objectives? *(check or cross)*	Does this help achieve the schools' objectives? *(check or cross)*
1			
2			
3			
4			
Identify any problems you see based on your observations and inferences.			

Formulating Arguments

8b – Gather and organize relevant information to formulate an argument.

8f – Recognize and evaluate propositions.

1.2m – Organize and depict information logically.

Mastery

You will know you are at the **Expert** level in the use of this ATL skill set when you can easily use relevant information to build a convincing logical argument taking into account both sides of any issue.

An *argument* is a structured discourse, either written or verbal, where evidence is provided to support a premise or series of premises which lead to a conclusion. Each premise is written in the form of a proposition – that is something which is either true or false – and then the evidence is provided to determine the truth of the premise. The logical sequence of truth will then lead to the conclusion.

Exercise 1 – Work your way through the table to create a valid argument

a) What is the subject matter about which you are developing an argument? Is it a topic for investigation, a question to be answered or a proposition or thesis to be defended?

b) What do you know to be true about this subject?

c) You build an argument to prove that a certain point is true. What is the point of your argument? What is the conclusion that your argument will support and to which it will ultimately lead?

If you are not clear about this before you start it is OK to research all aspects of the topic until you decide on your point of view and your conclusion and then build your argument to support your desirable conclusion.

d) What is the logical sequence of premises (claims, statements or propositions) which, if proven true, will lead to the desired conclusion?

e) For each premise, do your research and find the evidence that supports each premise and that which is contrary – that which denies the premise or supports its opposite

f) For each premise, develop an argument, a perspective, a specific example or a question that overcomes the contrary evidence and supports each premise

g) When developing your argument be very careful to distinguish between correlation and causality:

   i. Correlation is when two things occur together – useful to emphasise a particular point of view but does not prove any causal link between those two things

   ii. Causality is when you have proved that one thing causes – brings about – the other

h) Work with a partner and explain your full argument and your conclusion to your partner. Ask them to try to find flaws in your argument:

   a. "Yes, but …………"

   b. "What if …………"

i) If your partner was able to find areas where your argument was weak, go back and do more research until you can find data which supports your premise and your conclusion.

Topic description, question or thesis	
What do you know to be true?	
Conclusion to be developed	

Sequence of premises that will lead to the conclusion	Supporting evidence	Contrary evidence	Argument to overcome contrary evidence and support premise
1.			
2.			
3.			
4.			
5.			

Evaluating Assumptions

8c – Recognize unstated assumptions and bias.
8e – Evaluate evidence and arguments.
8g – Draw reasonable conclusions and generalizations.
8h – Test conclusions and generalizations.
8m – Develop contrary or opposing arguments.

Mastery

You will know you are at the **Expert** level in the use of this ATL skill set when you can easily recognize the assumptions behind statements and distinguish between valid and invalid arguments.

Assumptions are beliefs upon which we base the logic of our argument. They are the things we presume to be true without evidence. Our assumptions depend on our particular point of view, frame of reference and cultural perspective (e.g. is Canada at the top or the bottom of the world?) Does that depend on where in the world you live?

Our assumptions are made up of pre-suppositions – what needs to be true to make sense of our argument – axioms – what is self-evidently true and does not need to be proved, and things we take for granted – "common sense" or educated guesses about reality.

Exploring the assumptions within arguments helps us to determine the validity of the argument.

Exercise 1 – Recognizing assumptions

To understand the different parts of any argument, find a discussion of a controversial local or international event or an editorial in a newspaper in which the author is making a case for a certain conclusion, and then work your way through the following analysis:

a) Identify and separate out the premises, the evidence for each premise and the conclusion

b) Analyze each sentence or each statement separately, looking for stated assumptions like:

   i. global statements – as we all know...

   ii. group identifiers – well educated people would all agree...

   iii. generalizations – it is safe to assume...

c) Also look for unstated but assumed connections between statement or ideas. Look for:

   i. necessary conditions – in order for that to be true this has to be true as well

   ii. sufficient conditions – this always means that

   iii. cause-and-effect connections – this brings about that

   iv. sequential connections – if this happens then that happens

   v. assumed examples – this is an example of that

   vi. opinions stated as facts – "I think it is obvious that..."

   vii. consistent bias or particular point of view

   viii. any hidden agenda.

d) For each premise, see if you can think of something which, if it were true, would contradict the stated premise

e) Decide how valid or true you think each premise is

f) Can you think of a different conclusion to the one the author has stated which would better fit the facts as you see them

g) How do you think your own unstated assumptions or bias has affected your analysis of the argument?

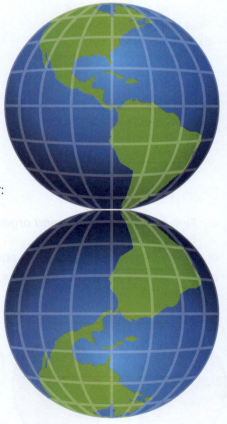

Conclusion of the argument			

Sequence of premises that lead to the conclusion	Analysis of assumptions		
	What needs to be true in order for the premise to be true?	What would be something that if it were true would contradict the premise?	How valid or true do you think the premise is?
1.			
2.			
3.			
What other conclusion could you draw from the facts as you see them?			
How valid or true do you think the conclusion is?			
How do you think your own perspective, unstated assumptions or bias have influenced your analysis?			

Exercise 2 – Draw reasonable conclusions

a) First go to **8b – Gather and organize relevant information to formulate an argument** (page 161) and construct your own argument and conclusion

b) Go through all the steps a) – g) above and objectively analyze your own process of building premises to support a conclusion

c) Do you think you have built a strong argument to support your conclusion?

Data Analysis

8d – Interpret data.

8r – Identify trends and forecast possibilities.

6g – Collect and analyze data to identify solutions and make informed decisions.

6h – Process data and report results.

Mastery

You will know you are at the **Expert** level in the use of this ATL skill set when you can analyze your data accurately and reach valid conclusions.

HOW TO INTERPRET DATA – KEY POINTS

1) Be clear about your purpose in collecting data – are you trying to be scientifically objective or are you trying to prove an already decided conclusion?

2) What kind of data do you have or want to collect?

   i. quantitative data – measurements of things that come in quantities like time, distance, weight, volume, temperature, number, etc.

   ii. qualitative data – what people think, or feel, or understand about something.

   Gathering qualitative data is sometimes easier than gathering quantitative data but it is also likely to be more vague and imprecise and much more difficult to analyze accurately.

3) Make sure you are clear about what you are measuring – usually you are looking at two variables – *the independent variable* – the thing that you, as the researcher, are looking to change – and *the dependent variable* – the thing that you are looking to be changed as a result.

4) Once you have your data you need to organize it into summaries, tables, graphs and/or charts to enable you to see all the data at once and look for patterns – what responses were the same or similar to each other and what responses were different?

5) Data analysis is all about looking for patterns – what goes with what?

   i. Graphical analysis will give you a visual representation of data and may well reveal a pattern – easy to do with spreadsheet tools

   ii. Statistical analysis uses mathematical tools to determine if there are patterns within data – simple patterns involving the Mean, Mode, Median and

Spread or Variability of the data – or more complex patterns using linear regression or correlation analysis.

6) When analyzing your data, be very careful to distinguish between correlation and causality:

   i. Correlation is when two things occur together – useful to emphasize a particular point of view but does not prove any causal link between those two things

   ii. Causality is when you have proved that one thing causes – brings about – the other.

7) Use statistical tools for analyzing all forms of data.

8) Be aware of significance. If a conclusion is significant, in statistical terms it means that it couldn't have happened by chance. There are different levels of significance – if you can say from your statistical analysis of the data that a relationship is significant at the 1% level that means that 1 time in 100 that result could have happened by chance so statistically your conclusion will be true 99 times out of 100. If the data is significant at the 0.1% level that means that 1 time in 1000 that result could have happened by chance, which makes your conclusion much more significant. For more information, see your math or statistics teacher.

9) Test the validity of your conclusion:

   a. Internal – if someone else repeated your study, would they arrive at the same conclusion? If so, then you have established *reliability* or *internal validity*

   b. External – would your conclusion be correct if applied to other people, other cultures or in other countries? If so, then you have achieved *generalizability* or *external validity*.

10) Trends and forecasts – there are many ways to look at the way your data changes over time and create what is known as a time series model. This uses inferential statistics to look at the way your data changed in the past and, by keeping some factors constant, tries to predict the way the same data will change in the future, in order to make a prediction. Some methods are:

a. Many spreadsheets and search engines contain trend analysis options

b. Graphically using best-fit or moving averages to extend a graph into the future

c. Mathematically determining a formula, or a rule for a relationship between two data sets, which is consistent in the past and can be used to predict the future

d. Linear regression and forecasting

e. Multiple factor optimization

The name of your research study	
What was your initial research goal?	
What patterns have you found in your data – what connections can you make between factors?	
What conclusions have you drawn from the data?	
Can you apply your conclusion to people other than those in your study? How might it be different?	
Can you apply your conclusion to other countries or other cultures? How might it be different?	
What trends have you noticed in the data?	
What predictions can you make?	
How certain are you of your predictions?	

Revising

Mastery

You will know you are at the **Expert** level in the use of this ATL skill when you become good at noticing:
- a) when you don't understand something
- b) ideas and information that challenge your present understanding

and you are comfortable in reviewing the evidence and changing your own understandings where necessary.

This ATL skill is the basis of all learning and starts with realizing what you don't know and then taking action to revise your understandings and create new understandings.

It would be useful for you to first do the three exercises in **1.2i, 1.2j – Note-making** on page 33; and the exercise in **4.5b – Practice "failing well"** on page 109 first.

The key to understanding (and remembering well) is putting ideas into your own words.

Exercise 1 – What's true for me?

a) Fill in the following table as a reflective exercise:

Something that I used to believe or think was true that I have changed my mind on these days was...

What changed my mind about this was...

What I now understand to be true for me is...

Exercise 2 – Gathering evidence

a) Then look at something that someone else believes or thinks is true that you disagree with, and evaluate the evidence for the claim by filling in the following table:

Something that you don't think is true...			
Sequence of premises that leads to the conclusion that you don't think is true	**Evidence for each premise**	**Evidence against each premise**	**Restate each premise as what you think is true**
1.			
2.			
3.			
What conclusion do you now draw from the facts as you see them?			
Have you changed your position in consideration of the evidence?			

Exercise 3 – Understanding school work

a) Identify something in one of your subjects that you don't yet understand (see **5e – Reflection on content** on page 116) and try working your way through the following table:

The thing that I just don't understand yet is...
The question that I need to get the answer to is...

The place I am going to check to see if I can get an explanation are: • a teacher • a friend • an older student • another adult • the textbook • the internet	What I found was:
My new understanding is (written in your own words)...	

Risk

8j – Evaluate and manage risk.

To get the most out of these exercises it would be useful to have first worked through ATL skill *4.5a,c,d Resilience* on page 107, *4.5b Failing Well* on page 109 and *4.4a,b,c Self-Motivation* on page 101.

Risk is the possibility of losing something of value. Risk management means accurately assessing potential risk and taking appropriate action based on that assessment.

Risk-taking allows a young person to test their limits, learn new skills, develop competence and self-worth, and assume greater responsibility for their life. But risk-taking behavior can be dangerous to health or safety when it is characterised or motivated by:

- ignorance (lack of experience of any similar action)
- impulsiveness or thrill-seeking
- lack of good information on possible consequences of behavior
- feelings of inadequacy and a desire to fit in

To assess risk accurately, you need to be clear about why you are doing something and then assess what the short- and long-term benefits and costs might be. This is called a cost/benefit analysis and needs good, accurate research and the consideration of facts not opinions.

Exercise 1 – Evaluate risks in teenage behavior

a) Try filling in the blanks on the following table for Example 1 – smoking cigarettes. Do the research and see if the costs and benefits outlined in the table fit with the research

b) Think of two actions that you haven't taken yet but that you are considering taking in the future and apply the same risk/benefit analysis to those actions.

	Example 1	Example 2	Example 3
Behavior	E.g. smoking cigarettes		
My purpose, reason, motivation	To fit in with other people who do this		
Personal cost	Money spent Bad breath Bad smelling clothes & hair Shortness of breath Lack of fitness		

Research on costs			
Immediate benefit	Don't feel left out		
Research on benefits			
Best possible outcome	I survive		
Research on best outcomes			
Worst possible outcome	I die at a young age from a disease like lung cancer		
Research on worst outcomes			
Make a decision – is the behavior worth doing?	No		
Why or why not?	No advantages, lots of disadvantages		

Protective factors can act as a buffer to the negative effects of risk factors and risk-taking behaviors. The most powerful protective factors in reducing morbidity among young people are connectedness and belonging to family, school and peers.

Exercise 2 – Manage risk

a) Imagine that you are thinking of starting up your own business washing people's cars at their houses on the weekend. Do the following analysis to determine if you are managing the risk well.

b) Then, either try analyzing Example 2 or write in one of your own. What is one action you are thinking of taking, something you would like to do but haven't tried yet?

	Example 1	Example 2	Example 3
What is the situation, behavior, action you want to take?	Start my own business	Go bungee jumping	
Define the risk.	I might invest a whole lot of time and money, and have the business fail		
What will be your investment?	100 hours thinking and planning time, $50 for bicycle saddlebags and cleaning gear		
What is the worst that could happen?	No one wants my service. I waste all the time and money I have put in. I strike an unexpected problem.		
What is the best that could happen?	The business is so successful I have to hire other people to work for me.		
What research have you done of the risks and benefits involved?			
Who else could you get involved who could share the work and share the risk?			
Who could you ask for advice about potential risk or if you strike an unexpected problem?			
If things did not go the way you planned what might be another option you could take that would make use of your investment in a different way?			

Everything you do contains risks – physical, emotional, social or intellectual, or a combination of factors – whether the risk is to you or to the completion of a task. Everything has risks. To learn to manage risk well you need to be very clear about what you want to achieve, analyze all pathways to achieving it for risk and then plot a path of action that achieves the goal while minimizing unacceptable risk.

Exercise 3 – Manage risk in achieving goals

1. Be very clear about exactly what it is that you want to achieve. What is your goal? Break that goal down into stages or steps.
2. For each stage, consider at least two different actions you could take to achieve it.
3. For each action, think of what would be the worst thing that could happen?
4. Decide if the risk is worth taking.
5. Plan out the best pathway to achieving your goal, take action and evaluate the result.

Fill in the table:

My goal is ....

The stages or steps necessary to achieve this are:	Two actions I could take for each stage:	What's the worst that could happen for each one?	What am I actually going to do?
1.			
2.			
3.			
4.			
5.			

6. Think about your risk management – how accurate and effective was that? What can you learn from the experience about effective risk management?

....

....

Exercise 4 – Manage risk in planning activities

1. What is the activity for, what do you want to do?
2. What are the possible risks? Do a full analysis of potential physical, social, emotional or intellectual risks to yourself and to any other people involved.
3. Evaluate each risk for danger to life and limb
4. For each risk, create an action plan to mitigate, avoid or work with the risk.
5. Run the activity and evaluate your risk management afterwards. What can you learn from the experience?

Fill in the table:

What I would like to do is..

All the possible risks are:	The danger of each one is:	How each risk can be mitigated, avoided or worked with is:
1.		
2.		
3.		
4.		
5.		

6. Think about your risk management – how accurate and effective was that? What can you learn from the experience about effective risk management?

....

....

....

Questions

Mastery

You will know you are at the **Expert** level in the use of this ATL skill when you can create good questions – of any type or order.

 Factual questions are questions about facts and evidence to back up facts.

 Topical questions are more to do with current events, questions about what is happening in the world – right now!

Conceptual questions are the "big picture" questions, looking for patterns in data, connections between facts and topics, ethics, influences, predictions, consequences.

 Debatable questions are simply questions that produce a mix of opinion or viewpoint, preferably into two opposing camps who can then argue with each other.

Exercise 1 – Good questions

WORK IN PAIRS

a) Take one current major International news story.

b) Imagine you are a TV interviewer and you have an exclusive interview with the key figure in this news story, but you are only going to be allowed to ask four questions:

1. One factual – how many, how much, how high, etc.
2. One topical – how might this affect your town, school, community, etc.
3. One conceptual – the significance or meaning that could be taken from this.
4. One debatable – any issue that people disagree about.

c) Write each question in the table below.

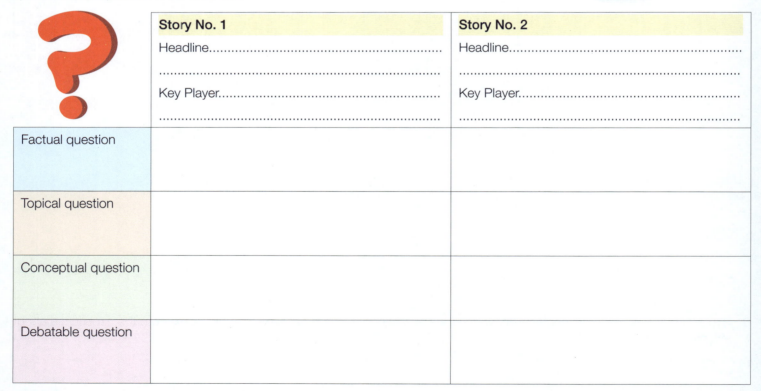

	Story No. 1 Headline.. .... Key Player..	Story No. 2 Headline.. .... Key Player.. ....
Factual question		
Topical question		
Conceptual question		
Debatable question		

d) Go through the same process again for a different news story.

Learning to ask good questions:

The best way to improve your performance in any area of your life that you want to change is to ask the right questions. Then you will get the information you need to make the changes you want to make.

Exercise 2a – Identify needs

What would you like to know more about? What would you like to be better at? What would you like to change? These are some of the things that you want to ask questions about. First you need to identify what you want to ask questions about and why, and then you can design the right questions to ask.

Fill out the table:

What would you like to know more about?	What would you like to be better at?	What areas of your life would you like to make a change in?

Exercise 2b – Identify resources

Take three items from the table above, the most important ones, and fill in the following table:

My three top things are:	My reasons for wanting to change each one are:	Where I could find more information about this is:	One person I could ask about each one is:
1.			
2.			
3.			

A good question:

- makes you think
- doesn't have an immediate answer
- requires some thinking, connection to previous knowledge
- demands more than a "Yes" or "No" answer
- interrogates information to find understanding

Exercise 2c – Ask good questions

We use questions to investigate sources of information or people in order to gain understanding and make meaning.

Use the table below to help you construct relevant questions about each subject from the previous exercise. Take one word from the left and combine it with each word across the top to design possible questions about each of your subjects from Exercise 2. Write in the boxes any questions that you think are relevant. Do the same thing with all the words on the left. See if you can write one good question on each row for each topic.

	is	did	can	would	will
Who					
What					
Where					
When					
Why					
How					

Exercise 2d – Find the answer

Use the questions in Exercise 2c to ask good questions for information. If that does not give you the full answer that you want, then you are going to need to ask the person you identified in Exercise 2b.

Think about the questions you want to ask and the direction in which you want the answers to go. Some suggestions for asking good questions of people are:

- Don't ask yes or no questions, ask questions that require a thoughtful answer
- Use the answer to one question to ask a follow-up question that digs deeper into the meaning or understanding you are after
- Use a pause and a look of expectation to draw out a more detailed answer to your question
- Don't interrupt any answer, allow the subject to talk.

Perspective

8I – Consider ideas from multiple perspectives.

Mastery

You will know you are at the **Expert** level in the use of this ATL skill when you can easily view any problem, issue, situation, event or piece of work from a number of different perspectives.

The more perspectives from which any idea is viewed, the more differing interpretations of that idea are created. Viewing any idea from multiple perspectives will enable you to consider all its strengths and weaknesses.

Exercise 1 – Great ideas

a) For each of the "big ideas" listed below, imagine that for all of your life, you have been living before this idea had been thought of, tested and put into practice in the real world. Imagine that this idea has been introduced recently and is starting to take hold in your world and things are changing as a result.

b) What things do you think you would notice change as a result?

c) Looking back from a modern perspective to the time of the introduction of this idea, do you think it had both positive and negative effects on the world?

	What changed as a direct or immediate effect of the implementation of this idea?	What are some of the positive effects this idea had on the world?	Were there any negative effects this idea had on the world?
Farming			
Evolution			
Electricity			
Feminism			
Human rights			
Personal computers			
World wide web			
Printing			
Money			
Cell phones			
Motor cars			
Aeroplanes			

Exercise 2 – At school

a) Imagine you were able to re-design your school and make it into the perfect school for you. What would you change?

b) If you were able to put in all the changes you wanted what do you think the impact of each change would be on teachers, administrators and students?

Things I could change are...	I would change them to...	I think the impact on students would be...	I think the impact on teachers would be...	I think the impact on administrators would be...	I think the impact on parents would be...
1.					
2.					
3.					
4.					
5.					

Problem Solving

8n – Analyze complex concepts and projects into their constituent parts and synthesize them to create new understanding.

8o – Propose and evaluate a variety of solutions.

8p – Identify obstacles and challenges.

8q – Use models and simulations to explore complex systems and issues.

8s – Troubleshoot systems and applications.

Mastery

You will know you are at the **Expert** level in the use of this ATL skill set when you are a good problem solver.

Finding the best answer or solution to problems requires the application of both analytical thinking, to break down the issue into its component parts and look at the evidence; and creative thinking, to generate multiple possible solutions or answers.

To find solutions and solve problems you first need to focus on thoroughly understanding the issue and becoming very clear about what the real problem is. Be aware that for many real-world problems there is not one magic solution, there is often a range of possible solutions; each of which may have positive and negative effects. The best solution is the one that, looking back from the future, had the most positive effect. Being a good problem solver means being able to pick that particular solution in advance.

Exercise 1 – Global and local problems

Get into a group of four and, as a group, work your way through the process of problem solving for Problem 1. Some of the answers are supplied, some you will have to generate for yourselves. Work through the table by following the steps below and filing in the gaps as you go:

a)   Gather all the facts – ask who, what, where, when, why & how?

b)   Define the real problem.

Problem 1	
Give the problem a name.	The unequal distribution of resources between people in the world.
What is the symptom of the problem that you have observed?	Many poor people, a few rich people in the world.
Do your research – what are the facts?	80% of the world's population survive on less than ($US) $10/day, 50% live on less than $2.50/day. Check these facts, find a reference.

Who?	
What?	What is the total $ cost of one day of your life? You might like to ask your parents for an estimate or try and work one out for yourself.
Where?	Where do the richest and the poorest people in the world live? Research, reference.
When?	When in history did we first get a separation between rich and poor people? Research, reference.
Why?	Why does a distinction between rich and poor come about? Research, reference.
Define the real problem – as a question	How can all people have equal access to all the world's resources?

c) Come up with one local example of this problem, or the consequences of this problem, that you have noticed in your local school or home community.

d) Brainstorm possible solutions – get a large piece of paper and write a description of the local example of the problem in the middle. Have everyone in your group take a pen and write anything and everything they can think of that might be a possible solution to the local problem on the page, all at once – for 5 minutes – no restrictions, anything is OK.

e) Working together, go through every solution written on the page and first eliminate the impossible ones. For each of those that remain, come up with at least one positive and one negative.

f) Weigh up all the +'s and –'s and decide on the best three solutions – you might want to do this by vote in your group.

g) Brainstorm again, this time trying to think of any ways in which each of your best three solutions could go wrong.

h) Choose your best solution and work through the next table:

Our local example of this problem is...	
Our solution to the local problems is...	
The obstacles and challenges we anticipate we will face in getting our solution happening are...	
How will we overcome those is...	
We will know we have been successful in solving the local problem when...	

i) Now you need to put in place the solution to your local example of the bigger problem.

j) Decide who will do what, how and by when, and how you will monitor progress in achieving your goal.

k) When you have everything organized and are ready to implement your solution to the local problem, be sure you make the solution process a loop where at every step you take action. Observe the results, learn from every result, make changes to your solution and take a new action.

l) Each time you learn from your experience, you may find that you need to change your definition of the problem as well – as you get closer to the actual, real problem.

Define the local problem	Action	Result	Learning	Changes
	1.			
	2.			

	3.			
	4.			

m) The last part of the process is "scale-up." Can you use your experience of solving the local problem to come up with a solution to the bigger problem? What might be a possible solution to the global problem as defined initially?

n) Fill in the last table.

One global solution to this problem is...	
The main obstacles to achieving this are...	
What would need to happen first for the global solution to be possible?	
What action could you take locally to highlight this problem and your possible global solution?	

Exercise 2 – Your own problem

a) Generate your own problem to solve from within a subject or from your community, family or social life.

b) Give your problem a name and work your way through all the same steps you took in Exercise 1.

Self-Assessment of ATL Skills

To see how best to use this page refer to pages 114 and 115.

ATL Skills	Novice Watch	Learner Copy	Practitioner Do				Expert Share
			Starting	Practicing	Getting better	Got it!	
Observing							
Formulating Arguments							
Evaluating Assumptions							
Data Analysis							
Revising							
Risk							
Questions							
Perspective							
Problem Solving							

Table title: **Student Self-Assessment of ATL Skills Proficiency – CRITICAL THINKING SKILLS**

Notes

CREATIVE THINKING SKILLS

Creativity is about generating ideas that did not exist before. Creative thinking skills are a combination of techniques that help you get into a creative state of mind and tools that you can use in that particular state of mind to generate new, original ideas.

Creative thinking requires open-mindedness, flexibility and adaptability in thinking and the ability to look at situations or problems from a fresh perspective and generate unorthodox, new, possibly even unsettling, ideas or solutions.

Creative thinking provides the necessary balance to critical thinking in the problem-solving process. Critical thinking looks specifically at what is and builds evidence-based arguments to enable a clarity of thought, focused only on the facts, in order to be clear about what is possible. Creative thinking is not bound by possibility and provides the thinking needed to generate previously untried, unconsidered, original solutions and ideas.

As Einstein is reputed to have said *"You cannot hope to solve any problems from the same level of consciousness that created them. You must learn to see the world anew."* All progress in human endeavour relies on creative thinking.

By practicing the exercises in this cluster you will get better at visual thinking, brain-storming, guessing, generating metaphors and analogies, and making unusual connections between things. You will also practice looking at situations, ideas and processes from different points of view and generating new ideas, improvements, novel solutions and original works. These are all the skills you need to become more creative in your writing, your design work, your art work and your thinking in general.

GREAT CREATIVE THINKERS THAT INFLUENCED TODAY'S WORLD

- ➤➤ Tim Berners Lee – the World Wide Web
- ➤➤ Steve Jobs – Apple, Pixar, NeXT
- ➤➤ Elon Musk – SpaceX, Tesla electric cars, Solar City
- ➤➤ Annie Leibovitz – photographer
- ➤➤ Karen Spärck Jones – information retrieval, IDF, search engines
- ➤➤ Mark Zuckerberg – Facebook
- ➤➤ Banksy – provocative, underground art
- ➤➤ Hedy Lamarr – actress and mathematician, spread-spectrum wireless technology
- ➤➤ Kathryn Bigelow – film writer, producer, director
- ➤➤ J. K. Rowling – Harry Potter series
- ➤➤ Stephen Hawking – physicist – black holes, quantum physics
- ➤➤ Yayoi Kusama – artist, novelist, poet.

Brainstorming

9a – Use brainstorming and visual diagrams to generate new ideas and inquiries.

Mastery

You will know you are at the **Expert** level in the use of this ATL skill when you automatically use brainstorming and visual diagrams to generate new ideas or questions.

Brainstorming is when you let your mind explore any connections you can make with a word or an idea. These can be freely associated connections or connections guided by a certain theme. There are no right or wrong answers when you are brainstorming.

When you record a brainstorm as an idea map, you are using words and images to generate a visual representation of the information. One image, picture or diagram can sometimes tell a story better than 1000 words. The source of our ability to generate new ideas, ones that have never existed before, is our imagination. Imagination can be developed through visualization exercises and practice in turning ideas and topics into visual diagrams.

Exercise 1 – Different brainstorms

You can brainstorm by yourself or in a group, on paper, out loud or using messaging.

What you are looking for in a brainstorm is connections, especially connections that your mind makes of which you are not consciously aware. The idea with brainstorming is to do it fast, without too much thinking, just saying or writing the first thing that comes to mind.

Try these different varieties of brainstorm:

a) Word storm – best done as an idea map – put five key words at the center of a page and from each one generate all the connections you can make with those words in a branching structure. Look for connections between the five categories of information.

b) Word association – same as Word Storm except you don't categorize the information, you don't look for connections. Start with a couple of key words and write down the first words that come to mind, and then the next and the next, etc.

c) Visual association – use images to stimulate individual words or a narrative.

d) Pros and cons – brainstorm the positive and negatives implications of any idea.

e) What if – change one variable and brainstorm the possibilities.

f) Imagine if – challenge yourself to see an issue from a different perspective, a different culture, a different time.

g) Ask questions – write questions, answer them yourself, generate more questions, as fast as possible.

h) Limitations – remove one variable at a time from the discussion – "What if we didn't have ... ?", "What if .... was constant?" Brainstorm possibilities, keep going until the problem simplifies.

Exercise 2 – Visual diagrams

a) Take one topic from any subject and turn the key points or main idea into four different visual representations including video and animation if you can find them.

b) Present all four visual representations to your class or your study group.

c) Ask your classmates to judge which one helped them to understand the main idea the best.

Topic:	Key Points:
As a diagram	
As an idea map	
As a flow chart	
As a single image	
As a video	www.
As an animation	www.

d) Which visual representation most helped you to understand the topic?

....

....

Impossible Solutions

9b – Consider multiple alternatives including those that might be unlikely or impossible.

9c – Create novel solutions to authentic problems.

Mastery

You will know you are at the **Expert** level in the use of this ATL skill set when you can easily generate novel solutions to authentic problems.

To complete this exercise well it would be an advantage to have first done *8n,o,p,q,s – Problem solving* on page 179; and *9a – Brainstorming* on page 186.

Exercise 1 – Other endings

Work in a group of four:

a)   Find one simple fairy tale or folk tale with which you are all familiar

b)   Summarize the plot of the whole story into a few short sentences

c)   Create four alternative endings to the story, one from each group member

d)   Out loud, each one of you needs to tell the fairy tale again with your own ending and ask for comments from your group

e)   Pick one ending that you all like the best and add more detail to the story until you have it in a form you can present

f)   Have one person tell your story to the whole class.

Name of the tale:		
Plot or storyline:	**Alternative endings:** 1.	**More detail on your best alternative ending:**
	2.	
	3.	
	4.	

Exercise 2 – Impossible solutions

Work in a group of four:

a) Use any one of the methods in **9a – Brainstorming** on page 186 to generate possible solutions to one current international or local problem

b) Encourage creativity – the generation of as many imaginative solutions as possible with no consideration of possibility at this stage

c) Analyze all the solutions generated and eliminate all the possible ones. Only leave those which you consider to be impossible

d) Choose your five best impossible solutions and work with those.

Describe the problem:

List your impossible solutions:	What makes the solution impossible?	What would have to be true for the solution to be possible?	If the solution did happen, what might be some of the consequences of solving the problem this way?
1.			
2.			
3.			
4.			
5.			

Connections and Ideas

9d – Make unexpected or unusual connections between objects and/or ideas.
9h – Apply existing knowledge to generate new ideas, products or processes.

Mastery

You will know when you are at the **Expert** level with this ATL skill set when you find it easy to generate many different connections between randomly chosen objects or ideas and use those connections to generate new ideas.

Two key creative practices are making novel connections between existing things and generating ideas that did not exist before. Both are skills that can be practiced and improved.

Exercise 1 – Connections between things

Work in pairs or as a group.

a) One person draws a line from one of the objects on the left to one of the things on the right

b) Everyone then has to come up with a connection between the two, and explain why, what is their connection

c) Discuss and choose which are the most logical and the most unusual connections and describe them in the last columns

d) Let a different person draw a new connection.

Connect one of these	with	one of these	Most logical connection	Most unusual connection
pencil		music		
sandwich		bird		
car		apple		
phone		tree		
television		snow		
table		marshmallows		
washing machine		happiness		
bed		elephant		
computer		dreams		
fence		time		
road		fish		
football		flying		
tennis ball		water		
school		space		
hospital		peanuts		

Exercise 2 – Connections between subjects

Work in pairs, find two school subjects you have in common, take one subject each:

a) Each person finds one topic in the subject in which they are interested, and writes down five key points in the table below

b) Then randomly link up one key point from the left with one on the right and work together on finding any connections between the two

c) Write down the most logical and the most unusual connections you come up with.

Subject 1...................... .... Topic 1 .... Key points:		Subject 2 .... Topic 2 .... Key points:	Most logical connection	Most unusual connection
1.		1.		
2.		2.		
3.		3.		
4.		4.		
5.		5.		
Connect one of these	with	one of these		

Exercise 3 – Most useful connections

a) Look down the lists of most logical and most unusual connections in exercise 1 & 2 and pick five that you think are worth investigating

b) Use each particular connection to generate new ideas of possible:
- machines or technologies
- apps or services
- games

by answering the questions in each column.

c) Do it for all five individually.

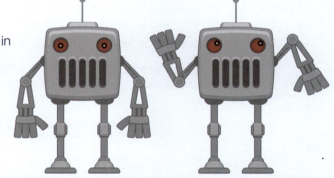

Interesting connections	What would be a machine or technology that could utilize this connection?	Can you think of a service that could utilize this connection? And maybe an app?	Can you imagine a game based on this connection?	What is one new idea that comes from these connections?
1.				
2.				
3.				
4.				
5.				

d) Looking at all the possibilities, see if you can use all the connections to generate one genuinely new idea, product or process.

Improvements

9e – Design improvements to existing machines, media and technologies.
9f – Design new machines, media and technologies.

Mastery

You will know you are at the **Expert** level with this ATL skill set when you automatically view all machines, media and technology from the point of view of form, function and possible improvements, and you can generate ideas for machines, media and technology that have never existed before.

This skill requires the application of two different types of thinking. One is a logical, analytical type of thinking required to break existing things down into their functionality and form. The other is a more creative type of thinking required to generate new purposes, new uses, new applications or improvements to existing things.

Two key, creative practices are making novel connections between existing things, and generating ideas that did not exist before. Both are skills that can be practiced and improved.

Exercise 1 – Mixing parameters to generate creativity

a) Work in pairs. Think of two existing machines (e.g. cars, washing machines, photocopiers, phones, etc.), two media (e.g. newspapers, TV, social media, etc.) and two technologies (e.g. email, messaging, face-to-face video, etc.) and write them in column 1.

b) Then analyze each one first by working horizontally across the table.

	How does it operate?	What is its function?	Who uses it?	What do these three have in common?
Machine 1:				
Media 1:				
Technology 1:				
Machine 2:				
Media 2:				
Technology 2:				

c) Then connect Machine 1 operation with the other two functions and see if you can think of a way that might be possible. Do the same for Media 1 and Technology 1.

d) Then connect Machine 1 functionality with the other two user groups and see if you can think of a way that might be possible. Do the same for Media 1 and Technology 1.

e) Do the same for Group 2.

f) Identify one possible new function or user group for each and write it in the next table.

g) Discuss how each would need to change to provide the new function or attract the new user group.

h) Describe the nature of the improvement and how you would know if it was a successful improvement.

	New function or user group	What would need to be changed to make it work?	How would you describe the improvement?
Machine 1:			
Media 1:			
Technology 1:			
Machine 2:			
Media 2:			
Technology 2:			

Exercise 2 – Using needs to generate new ideas

Either use the examples from Exercise 1 or generate two new machine, media and technology examples and, in pairs, work your way through the following table:

a)   What is one thing each one can't do? (e.g. A newspaper can't talk to you.)

b)   What is one thing you can't do with each one? (e.g. You can't use your laptop to dig your garden.)

c)   What would you like each one to be able to do? (e.g. Change the size of my phone whenever I want to.)

d)   What would have to happen for each one to be able to do this?

e)   If anything was possible, what would you imagine one new machine, media or technology would be like which was able to overcome any of the limitations and meet any of the needs identified in this table.

	What is one thing each one can't do?	What is one thing you can't do with each one?	What new function would you like to be able to use each one for?	What would have to happen for it to be able to do this?	A new machine, media or technology could be...
Machine 1:					
Media 1:					
Technology 1:					
Machine 2:					
Media 2:					
Technology 2:					

Guesses

9g – Make guesses, ask "what if" questions and generate testable hypotheses.

Guessing means estimating an outcome based on partial knowledge. In hindsight some guesses turn out to have been closer to the actual outcome than others. Learning to make accurate guesses is an important skill in many subjects.

"What if..." questions are great ways to either add or subtract an element of a problem or a situation to see how that would affect any possible solutions.

An hypothesis is simply an educated guess about a causal connection. It is a prediction of what you think might happen when something else happens.

Exercise 1 – Accurate guessing

Work in pairs, research and find two clips of important political speeches given by significant politicians, either current or from the past – don't listen to them yet!

a) Listen to the first sentence of the speech but see if you can stop the clip just before the politician finishes that sentence.

b) Both write down what you think the politician is going to say.

c) Play the rest of the first sentence.

d) See who was closest.

e) Pick another sentence, do it again.

f) Keep practicing until you are consistently guessing well.

Do the exercise again but this time use a movie clip that neither of you has seen before.

Exercise 2 – Mathematical estimation

Work in pairs, doing all the exercises in order. There are no right or wrong answers when you are guessing but the more you practice guessing well the more accurate your guesses will become. In Math it is always useful to know roughly what the answer might be so that you can see right away if a calculated result is in the right "ball park."

One at a time, do each exercise:

a) Run your eyes down the first column of numbers looking at each number for only one second and try guessing the addition at each step.

b) When you have both tried it, add up the numbers using a calculator and see which one of you was closest.

c) Do the same thing for all the columns.

	3		12		23		106
	8		9		46		357
	6		15		18		288
	1		11		54		620
	4		7		37		815
	6		18		92		131
	9		2		61		303
	5		7		75		782
	4		10		41		965
	2		13		89		336
	3		1		28		240
	5		4		13		682
	7		16		22		418
	8		6		74		527
	9		14		99		754
Guess							
Calculate							

Exercise 2 continued...

d) One person draws a line from one number in the first column to any number in the second column and the other person must immediately guess the answer and write their guess in the space.

e) Then you calculate the correct answer and write that in as well.

f) Then swap.

g) Keep going until you have used all the numbers once.

Are you getting better at guessing?

Do (d) to (g) again but this time use the numbers in the second column multiplied by the numbers in the third column.

h) Do (d) to (g) again using the 3rd and 4th columns.

Exercise 3 – What-if

In pairs, think of two movies that you have both seen and know well.

a) Think about the ending of the first movie and all the factors involved in that ending.

b) Agree on one factor to change and change it with a "What-if..." question.

c) Describe how you think the ending would change.

d) And then ask a "And then what if..." question and describe where you think the story might go.

e) Do the same thing for the second movie.

Exercise 3

	Movie 1:	Movie 2:
Describe the final scene of the movie.		
Who are the people involved?		
Think of one factor you could change in the story and change it with a "What if..." question	What if...	What if...
What would be some of the consequences of the change?		
How do you think that change might affect the final scene?		
Ask another "What if..." question.	And then what if...	And then what if...
What would be some of the consequences of the change?		
Describe how you think the story might have gone then.		

Exercise 4 – Generate testable hypotheses

An hypothesis is a prediction – When this happens .... I think that .... will happen.

Every hypothesis has two variables, the independent variable (the "this") – which is the thing that you, as the scientist, are going to change; and the dependent variable (the "that") – which is the thing that is going to be changed as a result.

In any experiment, what a scientist is looking for is a causal link – that a change in this, brings about (causes) a change in that. Which is quite different from correlation – where two things tend to happen together, but one doesn't cause the other.

In any experiment, there will also be a third type of variable – called controlled variables – which are all the things you are going to try to keep exactly the same in your experiment to make sure your result is valid.

The key to a good experiment is only changing one thing at a time and keeping everything else constant. Any change in your dependent variable can then be said to have demonstrated a causal link and you are in a position to create a new hypothesis or make predictions.

The heart of any experimental success is good data, which means measurability and control.

Fill in the blanks:

a) My independent variable is ....

measured in ....

and is able to be changed in the experiment.

b) My dependent variable is...

measured in ....

and is able to be measured during the experiment.

c) I can guarantee that changes in my dependent variable can only be due to changes in my independent variable by ....

....

....

d) All my controlled variables are...

....

e) My first hypothesis is that when I change..

I think ....

will change.

f) My result was ....

....

g) My new hypothesis is ....

....

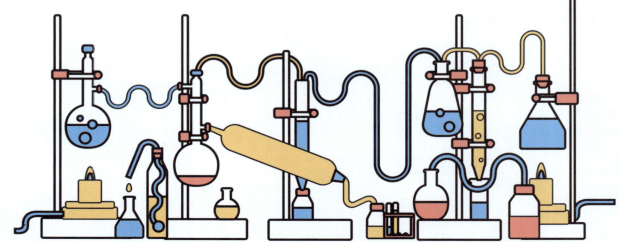

Original Works

9i – Create original works and ideas; use existing works and ideas in new ways.

Mastery

You will know when you are at the **Expert** level with this ATL skill when you find it easy to generate new ideas and create original works.

This skill requires the application of two different types of thinking. One is the observation and analysis of existing works, the other is the more creative type of thinking required to generate new ideas.

Two key creative practices are making novel connections between existing things and generating ideas that did not exist before. Both are skills that can be practiced and improved.

Before you do these skill exercises it would be useful for you to do **9d – Make unexpected or unusual connections between objects and/or ideas** and **9h – Apply existing knowledge to generate new ideas, products or processes** on page 190.

Exercise 1 – 100 uses

Divide into teams or groups or pairs or do it on your own:

a) As fast as you can, generate multiple uses for each of the objects in the table – as many different uses as possible as fast as possible. They don't have to be sensible uses or logical uses. Let your imagination come up with possibilities.

b) Try to get the full 18 uses for each one. It is only when you have to really push yourself for an answer that real creativity can break through.

How many uses can you find for a...					
brick					
paperclip					
pencil					
coat hanger					
candle					

c)   Describe how it feels to try to generate creative ideas when it feels like you have run out

....

....

d)   What do you do to get past that creative block?

e)   Now put the items together into pairs and see how many new uses you can come up with for each one.

brick and coat hanger					
pencil and candle					
brick and paperclip					
paperclip and candle					

Exercise 2 – State of mind

Being able to generate truly creative ideas – ideas that have never existed before – requires the generation of a certain state of mind, usually characterized by an increase in visual imagery and a reduction in internal dialogue – you stop talking to yourself inside your head. Being able to get into this state of mind when you need to generate creative ideas is a very useful skill to have.

a)   Practice the skill exercises in *4.1 – Mindfulness* on page 86 to learn how to monitor and gain control over your internal voice and get yourself automatically into a more creative frame of mind.

LAUNCH YOUR CREATIVITY

Flexible Thinking

9j – Practice flexible thinking—develop multiple opposing, contradictory and complementary arguments.

Mastery

You will know you are at the **Expert** level with this ATL skill when you can easily see every perspective on any issue or problem.

Flexible thinking is a style of thinking that allows for all possibilities, all points of view, not only in the discussion of ideas and the development of arguments, but also flexibility in the way we generate ideas and flexibility in what we believe about ourselves.

In order to practice this skill it would be useful to first do *8b – Gather and organize relevant information to formulate an argument* and *8f – Recognize and evaluate propositions* on page 161; and *8c – Recognize unstated assumptions and bias, 8e – Evaluate evidence and arguments, 8g – Draw reasonable conclusions and generalizations, 8h – Test conclusions and generalizations* and *8m – Develop contrary or opposing arguments* on page 163.

Exercise 1 – Who are you?

The whole of you is made up of many parts. When you think about yourself, are some aspects of yourself completely open to change and development, are some much more fixed, and are some somewhere in between?

a) Put a circle around one number from 1 (totally fixed and unchanging) to 10 (totally open to change and development) for each of these aspects of yourself:

	1 (totally fixed)				5 (50:50)					10 (totally flexible)
My mind	1	2	3	4	5	6	7	8	9	10
My beliefs	1	2	3	4	5	6	7	8	9	10
My memory	1	2	3	4	5	6	7	8	9	10
My intelligence	1	2	3	4	5	6	7	8	9	10
My personality	1	2	3	4	5	6	7	8	9	10
My body	1	2	3	4	5	6	7	8	9	10
My success	1	2	3	4	5	6	7	8	9	10
My ability to learn	1	2	3	4	5	6	7	8	9	10
My future	1	2	3	4	5	6	7	8	9	10
My knowledge	1	2	3	4	5	6	7	8	9	10
My life	1	2	3	4	5	6	7	8	9	10

There is no right or wrong here but, obviously, if you want to make changes and improve in any area of your life you first must believe that that aspect of your life is open to change, growth and development.

Exercise 2 – Multiple alternative explanations and arguments

a) Take some of the ideas we tend to take as facts and see how many alternative explanations you can come up with.

b) Then consider what would need to be true in order for each of your alternative explanations to be true.

Present "fact"	Alternative explanation			
	1.	2.	3.	4.
All stuff is made of atoms				
What would need to be true to enable each of your alternatives to be true?				
The universe started with a big explosion				
What would need to be true to enable each of your alternatives to be true?				
The earth is round				
What would need to be true to enable each of your alternatives to be true?				
The lights you see in the night sky are stars and planets				
What would need to be true to enable each of your alternatives to be true?				

c) Do the same idea generation exercise for four "facts" or conclusions from any one of your subjects.

Exercise 3 – Multiple opposing, contradictory and complementary arguments

a) For each of the facts presented above now do some research and see if for each one you can come up with any:
   i.   opposing arguments – that propose a different or opposite "fact"
   ii. contradictory arguments – that prove the original "fact" to be wrong
   iii. complementary arguments – that support the original "fact."

Present "fact"	Opposing arguments	Contradictory arguments	Complementary arguments
All stuff is made of atoms			
The universe started with a big explosion			
The earth is round			
The lights you see in the night sky are stars and planets			

b) Do the same idea generation exercise for four "facts" or conclusions from any one of your subjects.

Visual Thinking

9k – Practice visual thinking strategies and techniques.

Mastery

You will know you are at the **Expert** level with this ATL skill when you can turn ideas into images when you need to, and are able to work on those images, making changes, imagining other possibilities.

The essence of this skill is visualization – being able to imagine any possibility in your mind, clearly enough to be able to manipulate the image and create new possibilities. Some people find this much easier to do than others but everyone can learn how to visualize more effectively. Being able to clearly see your objective in your mind is a vital skill in all the creative arts.

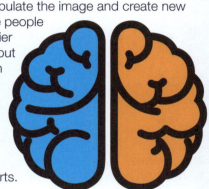

Exercise 1 – Manipulating images

Work in pairs. One person reads the text, the other person closes their eyes and imagines, then swap and do it the other way around. The text to be read out loud is in italics – read slowly, pause a lot.

a) *What does your front door look like? Can you picture that? What about your whole house or apartment. Can you imagine being able to see your whole house at once, as if it were just a model house? Picture it in isolation, by itself, against a light background.*

b) Pause, ask the person with their eyes closed to nod their head when they can see the image clearly.

c) *Now take the roof off your house in your mind. Can you see the top edges of all the walls, kind of like a 3-D floorplan? Move over the whole house until you can see the whole of the house from above.*

d) Pause, ask the person with their eyes closed to nod their head when they can see the image clearly.

e) *Now rotate the house in space until you are looking at the underside of the floor of the house, then take the floor of the house away too, so now you can see the framework of the walls again but from the bottom this time, against a light background. You notice that if you squash it all flat it becomes like a floor plan drawn on paper, the full plan of your house. So now you can fold it up, put it in your pocket and keep it for later.*

f) Eyes open now. Discuss the visualization, how vivid were the images, how real did it seem, how easy was it to make changes to the image?

g) Swap over.

h) Practice again. Visualize taking any machine or object (a car, a phone, a set of drawers, a hamburger) completely apart in your mind and then putting it back together again or transforming it into something else. You don't even need anyone else talking. You can do the whole process by yourself.

Exercise 2 – Memory castle

This is a visualization exercise that will help you remember information from each of your subjects accurately, and easily.

To begin with, work in pairs. One person reads the text, the other person closes their eyes and imagines. Then swap and do it the other way around. The text to be read out loud is in italics – read slowly, pause a lot.

a) *What you need to do first is imagine a fabulous house in your mind. The house that one day you would love to live in. The house that is a reflection of your character – it might even be a castle. See it clearly in your mind from outside, at the front. When you can see it clearly I want you to walk up to the front door and then open the front door and enter the house.*

b) Pause, ask the person with their eyes closed to nod his/her head when they can see the image clearly.

c) *You are inside the front door now, looking around. There might be a stairway to the upstairs, but notice that from this entrance you can see a number of closed doors leading off to separate rooms. And notice that there is a big label on each door and each one has written on it the name of one of your school subjects. What label do you see on the first door you come to?*

d) Pause, wait for an answer.

e) *OK. Now open that door and enter a room that is set up exactly as you would expect a room dedicated to the subject of .... to be.*

f) The person speaking has to now go through some things you might expect to see in that subject room, (e.g. if it is the Science room there might be books, tables and benches, microscopes and telescopes, chemicals, test-tubes and bunsen burners, a computer, some electrical machines and parts; if it is the English room there might be lots of books, magazines and newspapers, a computer, a stage, a writing desk, chairs, tables, etc). What can you see?

That visualization sets up the initial structure of your memory castle, all the rest of the work you need to do by yourself.

g) Individually, when you can, take some time to set up each of your subject rooms in your memory castle, in your mind – what you need to do is set up each room exactly as you would expect that subject room to be set up – a place where you could find whatever you needed to know in that subject. And make sure that in each room there is a big corkboard where you can pin up any important information.

h) Once you know what each room looks like on the inside, you can start using it to store your stuff. The trick is to store everything primarily as a visual image. If you can add sound and movement to each memory, that is even better, but first, all the memories must be visual. Once they are set up, you can use these rooms to store all the information you need to know to help pass your exams. All you have to do is put the information in the right place and then, when you need it, just go back to that place and retrieve it.

i) To put the information in the right place what you do is this. When you are studying, as soon as you have created some study notes, drawn a diagram, created a table or made an idea map containing information important to you that you want to remember, you need to look at it carefully, close your eyes and imagine it, then take it into your Memory Castle, open up the door to the room in which it belongs, go inside and create it there or put it there. Pin it on the wall or imagine it happening there. Represent it visually in some way and make sure you can see it there. Then walk out of the room, leave it behind and shut the door behind you. Do this for all your subjects and each time you enter one of these rooms look around and see all the stuff you have put there before. Then, when you have spare time, you can do revision in your mind by just taking a walk through all your rooms, reinforcing your separate memories in each room as you go.

j) What you are doing here is simply creating a separate memory store for each subject with lots of markers or reference points or connections to help you remember all the information.

Metaphors

9I – Generate metaphors and analogies.

Mastery

You will know when you are at the **Expert** level with this ATL skill when you find it easy to generate metaphoric and analogous connections between things and between ideas.

Two key creative practices are making novel connections between existing things, and generating ideas that did not exist before. Both are skills that can be practiced and improved.

 Spring Summer Autumn Winter

Exercise 1 – Using similes to generate creativity

Work in pairs or as a group.

a) One person in the group draws a line from one of the questions on the left to one of the objects on the right.

b) Everyone in the group has to come up with their own answer to the question and an explanation, if they can, for their answer.

c) Discuss and choose which are the most logical and the most unusual explanations, and describe them in the last columns.

d) A different person then draws a new connection and you repeat.

Connect one of these	with	one of these	Most logical explanation	Most unusual explanation
What color is...		Monday, Tuesday, Wednesday, Thursday, Friday, Saturday or Sunday.		
What animal is like...		Spring, Summer, Autumn, Winter.		
What fruit is like...		England, France, Italy, Russia, China, USA.		
What number is like...		Violin, guitar, drum, recorder, saxophone.		
What planet is like...		Beach, mountain, sea, sky, road, waterfall.		

Exercise 2 – Using similes to generate creativity

Work in pairs or as a group.

a) One person in the group draws a line from one of the objects on the left to one of the objects on the right.

b) Everyone in the group has to come up with their own answer to the question – "How is ... (object A) like ... (object B)?

c) Discuss and choose which are the most logical and the most unusual comparisons, and describe them in the last columns.

d) A different person then draws a new connection and you repeat.

How is one of these	like	one of these?	Most logical explanation	Most unusual explanation
rainbow		ice cream		
table		sunny day		
smile		vacation		
peach		snow		
feather		giraffe		
patience		whisper		
paper clip		lizard		
school		computer		
window		cold bath		
courage		banana		
rainy day		centipede		
vacuum cleaner		book		
honesty		bull dozer		
egg beater		gorilla		

Exercise 3 – Using comparison to generate creativity

Work in a group – notice that there are 12 rows of things in the table.

a) Three people in the group randomly choose a number between 1 & 12.

b) The first number chooses the question, the second number chooses one object from column 3, the third number chooses one object in column 5.

c) Draw lines between the three parts.

d) Everyone in the group has to come up with their own answer to the question, comparing the two, and an explanation as to why they have made that choice.

e) Discuss and choose which are the most logical and the most unusual explanations, and describe them in the last columns.

f) Three new people choose a number and you start again.

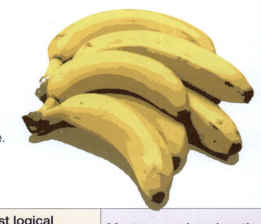

Use this question		to compare one of these	with	any of these	Most logical explanation	Most unusual explanation
Which is softer?		sleeping		table		
Which is faster?		summer		bathroom		
Which is smoother?		elephant		banana		
Which is funnier?		rainbow		gossip		
Which is louder?		success		winter		
Which is healthier?		feather		universe		
Which is bigger?		rain		hippopotamus		
Which is heavier?		happiness		snow		
Which is stronger?		idea		studying		
Which is more relaxed?		whisper		marching band		
Which is more honest?		cloudy day		piano		
Which is lighter?		deadline		door		

Self-Assessment of ATL Skills

To see how best to use this page refer to pages 114 and 115.

ATL Skills	Novice *Watch*	Learner *Copy*	Practitioner *Do*				Expert *Share*
			Starting	*Practicing*	*Getting better*	*Got it!*	
Brainstorming							
Impossible Solutions							
Connections and Ideas							
Improvements							
Guesses							
Original Works							
Flexible Thinking							
Visual Thinking							
Metaphors							

Student Self-Assessment of ATL Skills Proficiency – CREATIVE THINKING SKILLS

Notes

TRANSFER SKILLS

The reason ATL skills are so important is that they are the skills you need to learn well in every subject throughout your school life. From the simplest skills of bringing the right materials to class, concentrating, listening, reading, writing notes and working in groups, to the more complex skills of researching, writing essays and reports, developing arguments and problem solving – these are the skills that will help you to succeed at school, pass all your tests and exams, get good grades and achieve all your goals.

What makes ATL skills different from everything else you study at school is that while all your subjects change from year to year – get more complicated, more difficult to understand – the ATL skills you need to understand and do well in all your subjects don't change at all. ATL skills are the one thing that remains constant throughout your school life and also outside of school – when you go on to university or into a job. Anytime you need to learn anything new in order to achieve a goal you set for yourself, your ATL skills will come into play and if you have practiced these skills you will never have any difficulty learning what you need to learn and achieving all your goals. This is what is meant by transfer.

By practicing the skills in this cluster you will get better at being able to:

1) use your most effective ATL skills, strategies and techniques in any subject and in any area of your life where learning is important

2) use understandings gained in one subject area to make connections and provide insights into understanding other subjects

3) combine your knowledge, understanding and skills to solve problems or create new products.

GREAT TRANSFER – FROM OUTER SPACE TO THE KITCHEN

These are examples of ideas first developed for space exploration that were effectively transferred into useful products here on earth:

➡ Cordless drills – rechargeable batteries and low power consumption motors for use on the moon

➡ Smoke detectors – first developed to detect any potential problems in the Skylab space station

➡ Enriched baby food – high biological value algae-based foods for astronauts led to better baby food

➡ Ear thermometers – infrared sensor technology used to create disposable ear thermometers

➡ Teeth braces – nickel-titanium alloy wire now used with ceramics to make lighter stronger braces

➡ Protective paint – paint developed to protect the support structures of rocket launch platforms is now used to protect buildings, bridges and monuments

➡ Scratch-resistant glass – extremely hard coatings for glass and plastic lenses developed for spacecraft now used in glasses and industrial visors

➡ Comfy sneakers – shock resistant rubber used in astronauts couches turned into sneaker soles.

Strategies

10a – Utilize effective learning strategies in subject groups and disciplines.

Mastery

You will know you are at the **Expert** level in the use of this ATL skill when you automatically focus on the process you are using to learn to improve your understanding of your school subjects, and continually evaluate the effectiveness of all your learning strategies and techniques.

Another name for the process described by this skill is metacognition. Metacognition means thinking about your thinking – in this context thinking, about the strategies and techniques that you use to learn your subjects and how you can maximize their effectiveness.

Exercise 1 – What do you do at present?

To gain understanding of any subject matter you have to go through a series of processes – taking the information in, processing it until you understand it, storing your understandings. Each of these processes can be done a number of ways. You need to make sure you are using the best ways – the ways that produce the results you want in terms of learning, understanding and remembering.

a) First list all your subjects in the table below.

b) Then describe the processes you go through to understand each one:

i. How do you obtain the information? From the textbook, from the teacher talking and you writing notes, in a handout, from your own internet research, etc., or maybe a combination of things?

ii. How do you process that information to achieve understanding? Read it, make key point summaries, do lots of problems, do old exam questions, ask the teacher to explain it again, etc.

iii. What do you do with the information? Make idea maps, flash cards, diagrams, record yourself, try and teach a friend, find a related video, etc.

iv. What do you do to help remember what you need to? Make up acronyms, use associations, locations, connections, pictures, visual stories, metaphors, etc.

Subjects:	What are the main ways you obtain information in each subject?	How do you process that information to achieve understanding?	What do you do with the information?	What do you do to help remember what you need to?
1.				
2.				
3.				
4.				

5.				
6.				
What is one other possibility for each column?				

v. Write in one other possibility at the bottom of each column.

Exercise 2 – How do you know that your learning strategies work?

You can only ever evaluate and compare different learning strategies by trying them out in different subjects and seeing how easily and well you learn the material in each subject. To judge any learning strategy you need to think about its effectiveness – how thoroughly and well does it help you to achieve understanding of the subject matter, its efficiency. How quickly does it enable you to reach that understanding, and its memorability. How easy is it to remember what you learned and how long does that memory last?

a) Think of five different ways you could process information and learn school work (e.g. watching video, role playing, idea mapping, teaching someone else, flashcards, etc.), and try each one out with a different subject.

b) Then evaluate each one for effectiveness, efficiency and memorability and rate from 1 (the best) to 7 (the worst).

c) Now that you have tried each one, does any one learning strategy lend itself to a particular subject?

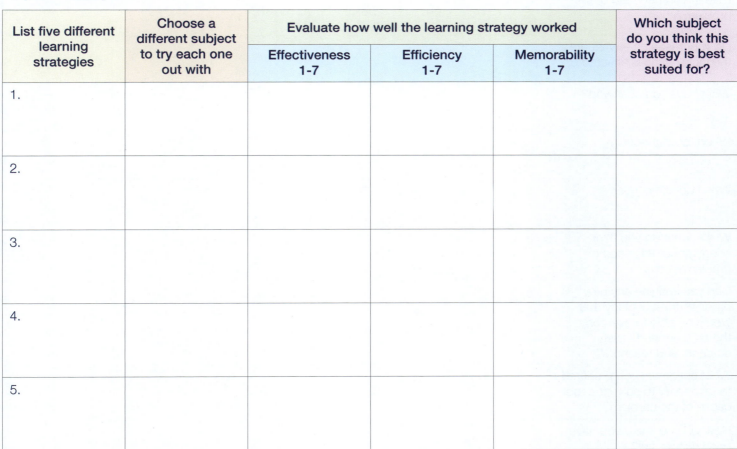

List five different learning strategies	Choose a different subject to try each one out with	Evaluate how well the learning strategy worked			Which subject do you think this strategy is best suited for?
		Effectiveness 1-7	Efficiency 1-7	Memorability 1-7	
1.					
2.					
3.					
4.					
5.					

Apply Skills

Mastery

You will know you are at the **Expert** level in the use of this ATL skill set when you automatically use all your knowledge, understandings and skills to view problems from multiple points of view and to solve problems and generate product ideas.

Exercise 1 – Perspectives on problems

From knowledge comes understanding and then action. ATL skills are involved both in turning knowledge into understanding and in generating action from understanding. This ATL skill is all about combining understanding and action to solve problems or create product ideas. First you need to find a real problem or an unmet need and then work your way through the following steps:

Work together in a group of 2 – 4.

a) Look around for a suitable example from your school of a need (or want) that you think isn't being met (e.g. to be able to use your phone in every class) or a problem that you think needs solving (e.g. lunch queues).

b) Work your way through this table looking at each question from both a student's and a teacher's point of view:

	Students point of view	Teacher's point of view
Give the unmet need or the problem a name.		
Do your research – what are the facts? Who is affected?		
What have you observed?		
Where does it occur?		
When does it occur?		
Why – what do you think brings about this need or problem?		
Can you imagine any new product or technology that would be able to overcome the problem and satisfy students and teachers?		
What action are you prepared to take to try to solve the root cause of the problem?		
How will you know you have been successful?		

Contexts

10c – Inquire in different contexts to gain different perspectives.
10h – Change the context of an inquiry to gain different perspectives.

Mastery

You will know you are at the **Expert** level in the use of this ATL skill set when you deliberately change the context of any inquiry in order to generate new ideas or find solutions.

To be able to use this skill, you will need to already be involved in inquiry learning – finding material through your own research to answer a question or solve a problem. The context of any inquiry means the circumstances that form the setting for an event, statement, or idea, the boundaries within which the inquiry will operate. Context can be geographical, political, historical, cultural, social, etc., and changing the context of any inquiry can create new perspectives which can then bring about new insights, new directions of inquiry and possible solutions to problems.

Exercise 1 – Changing context

Take any inquiry learning project or assignment with which you are engaged at the moment in any subject, preferably something you are finding challenging, and try changing the context of the inquiry to generate a new perspective on the question or the problem.

a) Describe the inquiry as the teacher gave it to you – what is the question you have to answer or the problem you have to solve?

b) Describe the context or setting of the inquiry – who does it relate to, where, when?

c) What have you discovered so far and what are you finding challenging?

d) Change each of the contextual factors in turn and consider the inquiry question or problem from a new perspective.

Describe the inquiry – what do you have to do?	
What is the context of the inquiry? Who? Where? When?	
What have you discovered so far?	
What are you finding challenging?	
If you changed the "who" – how might the inquiry change?	
If you changed the "where" – how might the inquiry change?	
If you changed the "when" – how might the inquiry change?	
If you changed any other contextual factor how might the inquiry change?	
Has changing perspective helped you to overcome your difficulties?	

Concepts

10d – Compare conceptual understanding across multiple subject groups and disciplines.

Mastery

You will know you are at the **Expert** level in the use of this ATL skill when you are studying one subject and you automatically make connections to conceptual understandings gained from other subjects.

All Units that you will be doing over your MYP years contain both Key and Related Concepts in their description. Key Concepts are the principles or ideas that represent the lens through which the subject matter is to be viewed. Related concepts are the principles or ideas that link the key concept to the particular subject matter. To practice this skill you are going to look for connections between Key Concepts within and across subjects, to look for patterns or overarching understandings that link all the Key Concepts.

Exercise 1 – Conceptual transfer within one subject

To do this exercise you will need to fill in the next table over one year.

a) Take any one of your subjects and, starting from now, each time you start a new unit write the Key Concept for that unit in the table.

b) Explain what you understand the concept to mean.

c) Find one example of the demonstration or application of the Key Concept from within the unit.

d) At the end of the year, look over all of the examples in the table. Look for connections and write an explanation or describe a concept or one example that ties them all together.

Key concept	Meaning	Subject Example	Connections
1.			
2.			
3.			
4.			
5.			
6.			

7.			
8.			
9.			
10.			

Exercise 2 – Conceptual transfer between subjects

To do this exercise you will need to fill in the next table over one year.

a) Write in all your subjects and, for each subject, any time during the year pick one unit and write the Key Concept for that unit in the table below.

b) Explain what you understand the concept to mean.

c) Find one example of the demonstration or application of the Key Concept from within the unit.

d) At the end of the year, look over all of the examples in the table. Look for connections and write an explanation or describe a concept or one example that ties them all together.

Subject	Key concept	Meaning	Subject Example	Connections
1.				
2.				
3.				
4.				
5.				
6.				
7.				
8.				
9.				
10.				

Connections

Mastery

You will know you are at the **Expert** level in the use of this ATL skill when you automatically notice connections between ideas occurring in different subject areas.

At school, you tend to learn all your subjects separately. But in order to make sense of the world around you, you need to be able to put all your different subject knowledge together. The important skill is in being able to view any concept, any idea or anything in the real world from the point of view of each of your subject disciplines. Learning to make connections between different subject concepts and ideas is a good way to practice this skill.

Exercise 1 – Connections between subjects

a) Write in all of your school subjects.

b) From each subject choose one big concept and one big idea and write them in.

c) Draw lines in column 3 connecting any concepts and ideas between which you can see a connection. Write an explanation of the connection along the line.

d) Can you see any pattern in these connections, any overarching concept? Do these connections generate any new ideas for you?

Subject	One big concept and one big idea	Connections and Explanations	New overarching ideas or concepts
1.	Concept:		
	Idea:		
2.			
3.			
4.			
5.			
6.			
7.			
8.			

New Technology

10g – Transfer current knowledge to learning of new technologies.

Mastery

You will know you are at the **Expert** level in the use of this ATL skill when you confidently use what you know to try out, explore and use effectively, any new technologies.

All information technologies involve the representation and processing of information. Lessons learned from exploring a new database, trying out a new app, using a new device, can often be used to help understand and use other technologies.

Exercise 1 – New technology

Analyze five new apps, two new social media platforms and one new device for:

a) Input – what type of information does it collect, from you and from elsewhere – written words, pictures, video, sound, GPS coordinates, other digital information?

b) Processing – what does it do with the information – store it, transform it into a different form, use it to find something else, use it to create connections between people, use it to try and sell you things, etc.?

c) Output – How does it give information back to you – words, pictures, video, sound, charts, graphs, scores, references, links, connections, etc.?

d) Rating – how useful is this new technology to you, what are its advantages and disadvantages?

New technologies	Input – what information does it collect?	Processing – what does it do with the information?	Output – how does it give information back to you?	Rating – how useful is this for you?
Five new apps – only one can be a game 1.				
2.				
3.				
4.				
5.				
Two new social media systems 1.				
2.				
A new phone				

Self-Assessment of ATL Skills

To see how best to use this page refer to pages 114 and 115.

ATL Skills	Novice *Watch*	Learner *Copy*	Practitioner *Do*				Expert *Share*
			Starting	*Practicing*	*Getting better*	*Got it!*	
Strategies							
Apply Skills							
Contexts							
Concepts							
Connections							
New Technology							

Notes

Index – ATL Skills

Index – ATL Skills

Index – ATL Skills

Index – ATL Skills

ATL Skills

STUDENT WORKBOOK

Notes

Notes